# YORKSHIRE HISTORY
## EARLY YEARS

# R E BATCHELOR, M.A.

**Other titles in the series**

**YORKSHIRE HISTORY** *Middle Years*
From Tudor Yorkshire to Eighteenth Century life in Yorkshire

**YORKSHIRE HISTORY** *Modern Times*
From the Industrial Revolution to the present day

**YORKSHIRE HISTORY** *Early Years*
Prehistoric Yorkshire to the Wars of the Roses

**LOFTHOUSE PUBLICATIONS**
**29 Ropergate, Pontefract, WF8 1LG**

# YORKSHIRE HISTORY

## EARLY YEARS

## R E BATCHELOR, M.A.

Illustrations by Moira McTague.

# About the Author

Richard Batchelor developed a keen interest in history as a boy at the King's School, Peterborough. This earned him the Munsteven Exhibition in History at St. John's College, Cambridge.

War service with the Royal Engineers took him to the Far East and to the Indian Army, then he returned to read history at Cambridge and graduated Master of Arts in 1950. There followed a further spell in the army, this time with the Royal Army Educational Corps. It was during postings to Carlisle, Catterick and to the Yorkshire Infantry Brigade Depot at Strensall that he was able to visit many of the places associated with the fascinating tapestry of northern history.

On leaving the army he made his home in York and from 1966 he taught history first at Granby Park School, Harrogate and subsequently upon comprehensive re-organisation, at the newly created Harrogate Granby High School, where his enthusiasm for local history proved infectious. The special course which he organised awakened many children to the richness of their northern heritage.

Copyright: R. E. Batchelor, M.A., 1985

ISBN 0900 370 653

Published by Lofthouse Publications,
29 Ropergate, Pontefract.

Printed in Great Britain by A. Wheaton & Co. Ltd., Exeter

# PREFACE

I was prompted to write this history for the girls and boys of Granby Park School, Harrogate, many of whom became keen students of local affairs. I am pleased that Moira McTague, a young colleague, has been able to illustrate it for me.

This book takes the story from man's earliest beginnings in a land not long freed from the ice up to the end of the Wars of the Roses. It describes the conquest of the North by the Romans, its colonisation by our forefathers, Saxons and Danes, the grim consequences of Norman rule and Scottish invasion and the peaceful reconstruction of the country under the kindly and expert eye of the monks. The development of trade in the Middle Ages is noted and we learn of the skill and business acumen of a Yorkshire wool merchant.

No work of this kind would be complete without reference to town life and to the part that religion played in the life of medieval man. The corporate spirit and religious conviction of the time are both displayed in the colourful homespun pageant of the mystery plays so much a part of medieval city life. These plays have been revived of course in our own day.

I hope that the story will prove interesting to other folk, both young and old who are curious about the history of Yorkshire. Few counties have such a varied and fascinating past as ours.

The Yorkshire Story is brought up to date in two further volumes. The Middle Years and Modern History.

Spen Lane,
York.

R. E. Batchelor

# CONTENTS

# MAPS

# ILLUSTRATIONS

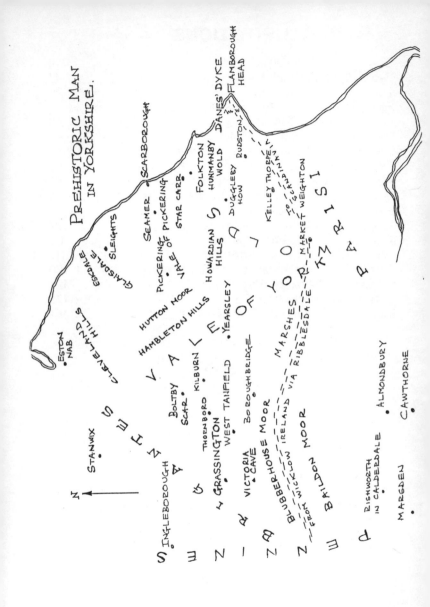

PREHISTORIC MAN IN YORKSHIRE.

# Chapter One

# EARLIEST BEGINNINGS

## PALAEOLITHIC MAN

No English county presents such a variety of scenery or such dramatic evidence of the work of man as does Yorkshire. There can be few counties with a more interesting history. To study this history we must go back in time to a date some 10,000 years B.C. when Palaeolithic or Old Stone Age hunters wandered from the Creswell Craggs in Derbyshire to find temporary shelter in Victoria Cave in the Pennines and in clefts in the limestone cliffs in Kirkdale.

The last of the four periods of glaciation had ended. Huge sheets of ice had cut the existing hills and valleys to their final shape and new surface deposits of clay, sand and gravel, dropped by the glacial melt waters, were slowly beginning to turn into the soils characteristic of the various regions of the county today.

But what of this early man? His tools were simple pieces of flint or stone roughly knapped into usable shape for chopping, boring or scraping. His quarry was the game living in the forest of birch, which was replacing the grasses and sedges of the earliest post-glacial period. His stay in Yorkshire was temporary for no evidence of permanent settlement has been found.

## MESOLITHIC MAN

Our next visitor was Mesolithic or Middle Stone Age man, of whom several groups entered Yorkshire independently from about 7,500 B.C. Some made their way along the shores of the much smaller North Sea, for Britain was then joined to Europe. Others who came may have come from the south,with possible links with people of Mediterranean or Pyrenean origin.

By now the climate was gradually becoming warmer and Mesolithic man, small in stature, could live on the unforested uplands, or by the open waters of meres by fishing and fowling, or by hunting red deer, wild ox, elk, roe deer and wild pig. All these abounded in the neighbouring mixed forests of birch, hazel and pine, now replacing the predominantly birch forests of earlier times. His tools were more cleverly made microliths or small flints sometimes only half an inch long, which he inserted into bone or wooden shafts, sometimes sticking them with glue made from resin deposits from birch bark. He had dug-out canoes, he hunted with dogs and he used the frontlets or skulls of stags in religious ceremonies to bring him good fortune in the hunt.

Evidence of the life of middle stone age man in Yorkshire is to be found in the remains of his summer camp, a lake dwelling at Star Carr in the Vale of Pickering. A platform of brushwood, built in the shallow waters of the lake shore has been preserved by a thick layer of peat which eventually covered the site. On this platform were found microliths, birchbark rolls and small worked bones. Mesolithic man probably sheltered here in dens made of tree branches or even in crude shelters made of leather. Later some middle stone age groups dwelt in the lower lying areas of the East Riding and, though there are no permanent settlements relating to this period in Yorkshire, we know that they wandered greatly, for their flint axes have been found as far away as Rishworth in Calderdale, Blubberhouses Moor in Wharfedale in the West and in Pickering and Glaisdale in the north.

Some Middle Stone Age hunters had a temporary camp near Marsden 1,000 feet high in the Pennines, where they manufactured flint microliths to be carefully inserted like barbs into arrow shafts. They travelled too, for their small worked stones have been found scattered in the Cleveland Hills and on the fringes of the North York Moors.

Finally Victoria Cave has provided us with evidence of a stag antler harpoon similar to those of the culture of northern Spain. Thus Mesolithic men in Yorkshire were hunters wandering in independent groups round the fringes of the forest and swamps, neither of which they dared penetrate too deeply.

# NEOLITHIC MAN

It was not until almost 3,000 B.C. that knowledge of farming reached Yorkshire, though small parties of farmers had reached the southern part of Britain some two or three centuries earlier. The farming practised was mixed. Cereal crops were grown and sheep, goats and pigs were kept. The art of pottery making began also in this period. Neolithic man avoided the valleys, for the heavier clay soils supported forests by now containing oak, elm, hazel and alder, hard-woods which he could not tackle. Neither could he drain heavier soils. The earliest farmers settled on the chalk downs of the Wolds and on better drained limestone soils and heaths wherever they occurred. There is no evidence of his settlement in Yorkshire to compare with such sites as Windmill Hill in Wiltshire, Haldon farmstead in Devon or Mildenhall in Suffolk. Pottery has been found at Beacon Hill, Flamborough Head, but evidence of Neolithic man in Yorkshire comes mainly from burial sites. These men made spectacular tombs. Their long barrows are to be found in eastern Yorkshire along the chalk wolds from Market Weighton to Folkton, and along the limestone hills north of the vale of Pickering from Sleights to Kilburn. They contain both inhumations, unburnt remains, and cremations. Skilful archaeological examination of these remains leads us to believe that the dead were often placed in mortuary enclosures and for a time exposed to the air. Later the whole area was covered over with a long mound of chalk or limestone to make a suitably dignified tomb.

By 2,000 B.C. later Neolithic farmers of different customs were arriving in the south. It was a long while before they reached Yorkshire where old and new customs now intermingled. At Duggleby Howe round mound we see a mixture of inhumation and cremation. Some remains are in individual locations according to the new custom, other groups indicate storage of bodies according to the old custom. Here also are seen fragments of Peterborough ware pottery, some flints identifiable as of Grimes Grave origin and some polished sharpened tools of more advanced craftsmanship.

# THE EARLY BRONZE AGE -
# BEAKER FOLK - METAL AND TRADE

Metal working was brought to Yorkshire about 1,800 B.C. by the Beaker Folk so named after the distinctive pots which they made, and which are commonly found in their burials. These people were probably of eastern Mediterranean origin, round headed and stocky. They arrived in Yorkshire from the Rhineland and Low Countries. They buried their dead singly in a crouched position and in round barrows. Their barrows are to be found all along the Wolds and on the lighter limestone soils. Occasional burials like those at Baildon Moor, Grassington and West Tanfield show their movements through the Pennine passes. Their importance was in their appreciation of amber, gold, jet, decorated pottery and fabrics. In their time there was a flourishing trade in gold from the Wicklow Mountains of Ireland, to the Baltic where amber was obtained.

One of the most revealing Beaker Folk burials was undoubtedly that of Kelleythorpe where a stone wrist guard for an archer, complete with gold rivet heads and some amber buttons was found. Other burials reveal golden ear-rings, stone copies of metal weapons and flints and iron pyrites for making fire.

# HENGES AND STANDING STONES

Between the Ure and the Swale, north and east of Ripon, are to be found a series of circular earth enclosures or henges and standing stones. These indicate that men were prepared to spend time and effort on work which would not give any benefit in food or shelter, and that society was sufficiently advanced to support large working parties in such building projects. Hardly anything is known of the strange and changing religious beliefs of this period, but the ceremonial avenue or cursus and the ditches and banks of the circles at Thornborough and Hutton Moor can be traced today. A standing stone remains at Rudston and the Devil's Arrows, three large stones in a field near Boroughbridge, stand almost 22 feet high for all to see.

# THE FOLKTON IDOLS

The Folkton Idols are three box-like images of hard chalk found at Folkton. Two of them with a stylised human face ornament with raised eyebrow design are thought to represent mother goddesses. The pattern of their decoration is similar to others found in Spain and Portugal. The third has decoration depicting the butterfly, a sacred symbol of ancient Greece. They were found in a burial barrow and are rare examples of their kind. It is possible that they may be images used for worship of the mother goddess Earth, giver of grain and nourishment. Not much is understood of the ceremonies or devotions performed to these idols, but beneath the barrow was the remains of a child perhaps five or six years old at the time of death. Could this be evidence of human sacrifice? Such things were not uncommon in the Bronze Age cultures of the Eastern Mediterranean. Associated with the people of the same period of pre-history are finds of flat stones with cup shaped hollows worked in them. These hollows may also have had religious significance, perhaps being used for pouring libations of drink, milk or beer, to the goddess of fertility or to other gods.

# THE MIDDLE AND LATE BRONZE AGE

Early Bronze Age man in Yorkshire favoured the light soil and the drier land. The bronze tools he used were most likely imported. The Middle and Late Bronze Ages were periods of expansion and improvement. Better tools and weapons were brought into use and scratch-ploughs, similar to those already in use in the south,may have been used in Yorkshire. The farm settlement at Crown End near Castleton in Eskdale has well defined embanked enclosures and field walls, cleared plots, grain storage pits and burial cairns indicating a more advanced agriculture and a more settled life.

Bronze smiths of this period were also more skilful. A bronze founder's hoard found at Yearsley contained bronze castings of advanced design made in two-part moulds. There were axe heads with stop ridges and flanges, socketed spearheads, rapier-like swords, sickles and even cauldrons made with riveted sheets.

The Folkton Idols

# THE IRON AGE

By 500 B.C. the first Celtic immigrants from Europe arrived on the coast of Yorkshire near Scarborough where numbers of their storage pits have been excavated under the Roman signal station. In the parts of Britain where the soils were suitable they were now worked by the two-ox plough with iron ploughshare. In other regions, notably the north, pastoral farming, horse breeding and cattle ranching were practised, as can be deduced from systematic examination of such sites as Staple Howe.

The Celts were skilful workers in metal, clay and stone and there was a flourishing trade in their time in metals and grain with Europe. The Parisi, immigrants of the La Tene Culture of the region between Paris and Burgundy, settled in the south east of Yorkshire,joining the loose association of tribes known as the Brigantes and probably bringing with them skill in chariot warfare. Certainly chariot burials were found at Hunmanby in the Wolds and at Seamer and Cawthorne, suggesting an organised society with nobles and common men. It was a turbulent period. Tribes were led by Chieftains and until the Roman invasions there was little common purpose and much inter-tribal warfare. The first century A.D. was a period of hill forts like Boltby Scar, Dane's Dyke, Castleton Rigg, Eston Nab, Almondbury and Ingleborough. Forts were not in continuous occupation but served as points of refuge in time of war. They were to fall to the Romans.

A Chariot

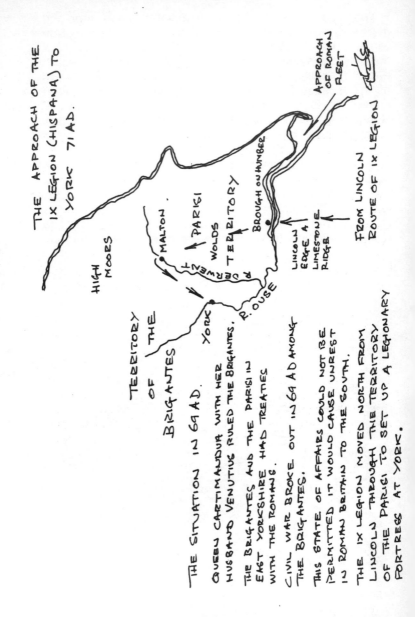

THE APPROACH OF THE
IX LEGION (HISPANA) TO
YORK 71 A.D.

HIGH MOORS

TERRITORY OF THE BRIGANTES

YORK

MALTON

PARISI

WOLDS

PARISI TERRITORY

R. OUSE

R. DERWENT

BROUGH ON HUMBER

APPROACH OF ROMAN FLEET

LINCOLN EDGE A LIMESTONE RIDGE

FROM LINCOLN
ROUTE OF IX LEGION

THE SITUATION IN 69 A.D.

QUEEN CARTIMANDUA WITH HER
HUSBAND VENUTIUS RULED THE BRIGANTES.

THE BRIGANTES AND THE PARISI IN
EAST YORKSHIRE HAD TREATIES
WITH THE ROMANS.

CIVIL WAR BROKE OUT IN 69 A.D. AMONG
THE BRIGANTES.

THIS STATE OF AFFAIRS COULD NOT BE
PERMITTED. IT WOULD CAUSE UNREST
IN ROMAN BRITAIN TO THE SOUTH.

THE IX LEGION MOVED NORTH FROM
LINCOLN THROUGH THE TERRITORY
OF THE PARISI TO SET UP A LEGIONARY
FORTRESS AT YORK.

# Chapter Two

# THE ROMAN CONQUEST
# THE INVASION

In 43 A.D. the Roman Army under an able General, Aulus Plautius, invaded Britain. Their aim was to conquer it, to exploit its grain and mineral resources and to extend and secure the northernmost frontiers of the Empire. In the early stages of the invasion the Emperor Claudius visited the advancing troops, set his stamp upon the conduct of the campaign and then returned to Rome to celebrate a 'Triumph.' By 48 A.D. the second Governor of Britain, Ostorius Scapula,had secured the conquest as far north as the Midlands and all the lowland area of Britain was in Roman hands. There was still resistance from the Ordovices and Silures of Wales however, and from the loose confederation of tribes dominated by the Brigantes of the north. It had taken the Romans four years to subdue the south. It was to be thirty years before the north was secured.

Before his attack on Wales Ostorius came to terms with the Brigantes. His campaign was successful and the Silures were beaten at least for a time. Caractacus, a prince of the Trinovantes, who had left Colchester to lead the Silures was now forced to seek refuge among the Brigantes. However, Cartimandua the Queen of the Brigantes, instead of granting him refuge, handed him over in irons to the Roman authorities in 5l A.D. This action led to civil war within the Brigantian federation the anti-Roman party being led by Venutius, Cartimandua's husband. At the Queen's request the Romans intervened, Cartimandua was saved and an uneasy peace followed among the tribes until 69 A.D.

The pretext for civil war this time was a domestic scandal. Cartimandua abandoned her husband in favour of young Vellocatus, his armour bearer, and again appealed to the Roman Governor for help. She was removed to safety,never again to influence affairs. Under Venutius the Brigantes and their allies hastily added finishing touches to their enormous seven hundred-acre stronghold at Stanwick, some five miles north of the road junction now known as Scotch Corner. The Roman administration accepted the challenge and the Ninth Legion moved from Lincoln to York on orders given by its former commander Quintus Petilius Cerialis who was now Governor of Britain. The campaign which followed was short and sharp. The Brigantes were attacked before their defences were complete and the Roman victory was decisive. The Governor pressed his advantage.The Twentieth Legion, which had replaced the Ninth at Lincoln, was moved to Chester and the stage was set for final pacification of Wales and the North. This was accomplished so successfully that by 80 A.D. the new Governor Agricola could campaign in Scotland confident that the territory in his rear was safely held.

# THE ROMAN ARMY

The Roman Army was quite different from the forces of the tribes opposing it in Britain. The Brigantes' organisation in battle was flexible and their tactics were designed for cavalry and chariot warfare which was spontaneous and impulsive rather than scientific. By contrast the Romans were masters in the science of war. The standard fighting formation of the Roman Army was the Legion with its supporting cavalry force - the equivalent perhaps of a modern army division. It was commanded by an officer known as a Legate,assisted by a Prefect and six subordinate officers known as Tribunes. There were some five to six thousand troops in the Legion,depending upon whether the centuries were up to strength. They were divided into six cohorts, each of ten centuries. The centuries were coupled to form maniples. The officers in close control of the troops were the sixty Centurions. These were long-service experienced soldiers. The more experienced of the two Centurionsof the maniple managed the two centuries on the battlefield. The legionaries fought according to a well-known battle drill. This gave them a tremendous advantage over less well trained tribesmen.

Each legion had its own baggage wagons, workshops, doctors, medical orderlies and clerks. There were all kinds of skilled tradesmen among the soldiers: armourers, blacksmiths, stonemasons, carpenters and wheelwrights. There was virtually nothing a legion could not do for itself. All the soldiers were volunteers and Roman citizens and therefore of some status. They served normally for twenty years and then retired as veterans with a pension, some savings and often a grant of land. The soldier's uniform and accoutrements were a coloured leather tunic, shorts or a kilt, armour made of strips of bronze, a bronze-plated leather belt, a short stabbing sword and dagger, some throwing darts, a bronze helmet, a long shield which would interlock with others, and a javelin. The soldier also carried a spade and other camp 'impedimenta.' Perhaps the most striking and upright young soldiers were chosen to bear the standards. There was a standard for each maniple and cohort and the standard in the charge of the first cohort was the standard of the legion. This was a pole surmounted by an eagle grasping in its talons Jove's thunder-bolts. Down the shaft of the standard would be a series of medallions proclaiming the 'honours' of the legion. Luccius Duccius Ruffinus, a soldier from the Voltinian tribe, bore one of the standards of the Ninth Legion. He died in York aged 28 and is portrayed on his fine tombstone in leopard-skin head dress and cloak.

The legions were supported by the auxiliaries. These were the troops conscripted from native tribes all over the Roman Empire. They were allowed to keep their traditional weapons but their tactics had to fit in with the needs of the legions. They never served in the areas where they were born, but were posted to other parts of the Empire. In this way they always fought against strangers and so remained loyal to their Roman Officers. Auxiliaries known to have served in the north of Britain were the Nervii and the Tungrians from Belgium, the Batavii from Holland, the Asturians and Vardulli from Spain, the Dalmations and Ulpians from the Balkans and even archers from Syria. At the end of his service an auxiliary soldier was honourably discharged and made a Roman Citizen. His marriage was legalised and his children became citizens. This was no small reward. The facts were recorded on bronze military diplomas,one of which was found at Stannington near

Sheffield. The retiring soldier would be presented with his own diploma and the duplicate would be sent to Rome for the archives.

Auxiliaries were usually organised into cohorts of infantry about a thousand strong or alae or wings of cavalry about five hundred strong. In pitched battle they were used on the flanks of the legions or as a screen in front. At other times they were used as garrison troops on such static defences as Hadrian's Wall. In peace-time they formed patrols to aid the civil government to police the country. This was their duty in Yorkshire supervising the Brigantes.

# THE FORTRESS AT EBORACUM

The ninth Legion crossed the Humber near Brough in 71 A.D. The site chosen for the Fortress of Eboracum commanded the main natural crossing-point of the Vale of York from east to west. From it, communications could be developed to north and south. It could be supplied with grain, oil, wine and iron by sea and with lead, stone and slate by river.

The first fortress was an earthwork. An area of some fifty acres, rectangular in shape and with rounded corners, was stripped of turf. Fresh-cut branches were laid down as a foundation all round the perimeter. Earth dug from the surrounding ditch was thrown-up inside on to the foundation of branches and the resulting bank was faced with turves. Inside the area the soldiers set up their tents, their headquarters and all the essential buildings of a fortress. These buildings were steadily improved and rebuilt in permanent form as time went on.

During Agricola's Governorship about 80 A.D., more permanent defences were built. Foundations of oak were put in over the first earthwork and the bank was raised with the earth from a new double ditch. The defences were held firm with turves and then surmounted by a timber palisade with interval towers. Fragments of these defences are still dug out today when building work is done in the city. In 107-8 A.D. in the reign of the Emperor Trajan, work on stone gate-houses and towers and on a stone wall built forward of the earthwork was commenced and the inner ditch was filled in. Part of the magnificent stone inscription taken from the south east gateway of the fortress and dating this work is to be seen in the Yorkshire Museum today. The perfect proportions of its lettering and the skill with which it has been carved are a tribute to the craftsmanship of the men of the Ninth Legion who built this part of the defences. Later in the second century A.D., when the Ninth Legion had been replaced in York by the Sixth the whole outer defences were again rebuilt in stone on more secure foundations of beaten clay, elm piles, cobbles and flagstones.

The final rebuilding took place late in the third and early in the fourth centuries A.D. There had been civil war in Britain. Carausius, commander of the fleet, and later Allectus, who murdered him, had both in turn declared themselves Emperor of Britain. The Emperor Constantius Chlorus defeated Allectus in the south in 296 A.D. However, the tribes of the north had broken out in revolt and this had to be suppressed. Constantius Chlorus came north and gave orders to reconstruct the permanent defences of the fortress at York. On the river front six projecting stone interval towers were built and two imposing multangular corner bastions. The Porta Praetoria or main gate was also strengthened with projecting semi circular corner towers. The walls along the east side were reconstructed and a red tile band was inserted to give strength and to serve as decoration. Constantius Chlorus died in York in 306 A.D. and his son Constantine was proclaimed Emperor in York. Such stirring events underlined the importance of the fortress and city as headquarters of the Government in the north.

# THE MILITARY ROADS

The Romans could never have held the north without a network of military roads linking forts and signal towers throughout the whole area. The basic network of roads was commenced at once and extended under Agricola. One road led from Doncaster north to Tadcaster then to York. From here it passed on through the Vale of York to Aldborough and Scotch Corner. There it forked, one branch going north to Corbridge and the other passing west through the Stainmore Pass to Brougham in the Eden Valley and then on to Carlisle. On the western side of the Pennines a main road ran from Chester, fortress of the Twentieth Legion, north to join the Carlisle road at Brougham. These main arteries were linked in several places through the Pennine Dales and over high passes. Modern roads follow their course in part today. Elsewhere in such desolate places as Blackstone Edge their abandoned pavements can still be seen. The eastern part of Yorkshire was served by a main road from York to Malton and then through the Vale of Pickering and on over Goathland Moor to a place near Whitby where there was a series of signal towers along the coast. This road was to gain importance when the Saxon raids began.

At intervals conveniently situated for marching were the forts which could house the auxiliary soldiers whose task it was to patrol the whole area watching, listening and controlling the movement of the tribes.

In time of peace the roads were the main arteries of trade. Merchants, travellers and envoys from all over the Empire passed over them north to Hadrian's Wall, to the Antonine Wall and further still to the very end of the civilised world. Britain was a province of the Roman Empire.

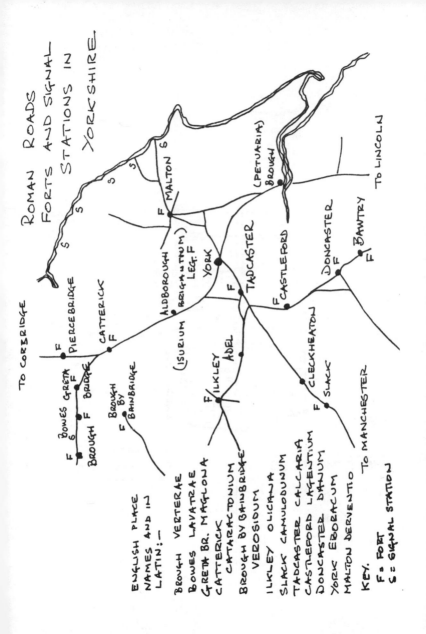

ROMAN ROADS
FORTS AND SIGNAL
STATIONS IN
YORKSHIRE.

TO CORBRIDGE

PIERCEBRIDGE F
CATTERICK F

BOWES S
GRETA F
BROUGH F BRIDGE F

BROUGH BY
BAINBRIDGE F

ALDBOROUGH
(ISURIUM BRIGANTIUM)
LEG. F
YORK F

MALTON S
S S S S S

(PETUARIA)
BROUGH

TADCASTER
CASTLEFORD F

DONCASTER F
BAWTRY F

ILKLEY F
ADEL

CLECKHEATON
SLACK F

TO MANCHESTER

TO LINCOLN

ENGLISH PLACE
NAMES AND IN
LATIN :-

BROUGH          VERTERAE
BOWES           LAVATRAE
GRETA BR.       MAGLONA
CATTERICK       CATARACTONIUM
BROUGH BY BAINBRIDGE
                VEROSIDUM
ILKLEY          OLICANA
SLACK           CAMULODUNUM
TADCASTER       CALCARIA
CASTLEFORD      LAGENTIUM
DONCASTER       DANUM
YORK            EBORACUM
MALTON          DERVENTIO

KEY :
F = FORT
S = SIGNAL STATION

25

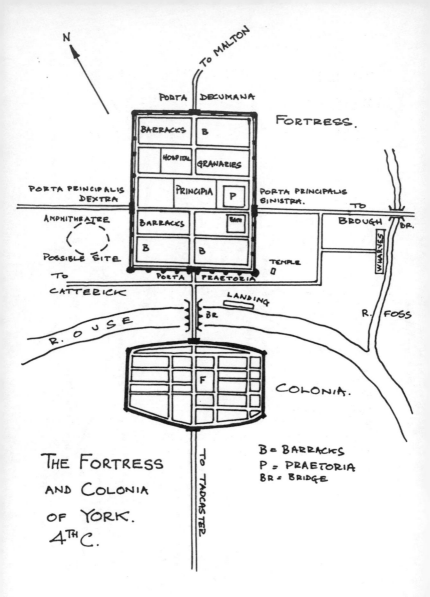

THE FORTRESS AND COLONIA OF YORK. 4TH C.

B = BARRACKS
P = PRAETORIA
BR = BRIDGE

# Chapter Three

# TOWN LIFE IN ROMAN BRITAIN
# THE COLONIA AT EBORACUM
# ROMAN TOWNS AS TRIBAL CENTRES

In the south of Britain life in large communities was not new to the tribes. They had lived together in times of danger in hill forts. As soon as the advantages of town life in settled conditions became apparent, they came to settle in Roman towns astride the new roads or at convenient river crossings. These towns became important tribal centres and the centres of civil government.

## THE FIRST ROMAN TRIBAL TOWNSHIPS IN YORKSHIRE

It was almost a hundred and fifty years before Petuaria or Brough on Humber, the main centre of the Parisi, became recognisable as a Roman Town. Throughout most of Yorkshire, geographical conditions favoured pastoral farming rather than grain growing to feed townsfolk. Most people lived in remote villages and farmsteads. Their main contact with Romans was the occasional visit of a detachment of auxiliary soldiers which accompanied the tax collector, for everyone in the Empire paid tribute to Caesar.

Later, Isurium Brigantium was developed north of York as a regional capital for the Brigantes. It was a large settlement covering fifty-five acres and surrounded by stone walls with towers for artillery. It had timber-framed houses standing on stone footings. Several of these houses had fine mosaic floors of great beauty which can still be seen. Many had a hypocaust system of under-floor central heating by warm air. By the west gate of the town there was a public bath house. Clearly Isurium was a civilised place in which to live.

Further to the north at Catterick lay the town of Cattaractonium by the banks of the river Swale which flows there like a shallow cataract. This town had shops, workshops, a public fountain and water supply, a bath house but no defensive walls until late in the third century A.D. A real effort was being made in the north to persuade the tribes to accept and enjoy the same advantages of civilised town life that were enjoyed by the people of the south.

# CIVIL SETTLEMENTS NEAR FORTS

Perhaps the greatest centres of Roman influence were the civil settlements which grew-up outside almost every Roman fort and, in particular, that settlement outside the legionary fortress at York. When six thousand soldiers, all being regularly paid, are settled in a permanent garrison they are soon joined by wives, families and civilian administrators. They and their families are served by merchants, entertainers, traders and craftsmen of all kinds.

# THE COLONIA AT YORK

The settlement at York started as a huddle of wooden or wattle and daub boths by the quays on the River Ouse and the River Foss, where ships came from other parts of Britain and from Gaul. Building soon spread to the area where the bridge took the main road from Tadcaster over the river into the Fortress. Here better brick and stone houses were put up and by the end of the second century York had become a self governing municipium or town. By 237 A.D. the settlement had grown sufficiently great in importance to be re-built as a planned city and to be officially granted the title and privileges of a Colonia by the Emperor Severus. We know this because Marcus Aurelius Lunaris, a citizen of York and a priest of the Imperial Cult, during a journey from York to Bordeaux made a vow to raise an altar as a thanksgiving to the gods for his safe passage. He carried out his vow setting up the altar at Bordeaux during the Consulate of Perpetuus and Cornelianus in 237 A.D. The altar was discovered in 1921 and is very ornate. The Colonia of York is represented by a boar carved in relief. On another side of the altar is the God of the River Garonne. Marcus Aurelius Lunaris is himself depicted sacrificing to a Goddess. She is seated and holds a cornucopia or horn of plenty. On her right is a bull, later to be sacrificed. The inscription on the altar proudly proclaims that the Colonia at York had become the capital of Britannia Inferior as the north was called.

The colonia was to the south west of the fortress and facing it across the river. It was walled and entry was by stone gate houses. The medieval walls surrounding the city today follow the course of the Roman walls in some places. Recent excavation of roads has suggested that the principal gate was close to Micklegate Bar where the Tadcaster road now enters the city.

Roman Forum

The Colonia was laid-out with straight roads intersected by side roads at right angles. Along the streets were the colonnaded entrances of houses and shops. There were public fountains from which householders could draw fresh water. The chief public buildings were to be found in the forum which stood in the centre of the town and there were public baths, temples, shrines and statues to commemorate the lives of the important people.

# EVIDENCE FROM BURIALS

The valley of the River Ouse is liable to flood and the colonia was built on an area of higher ground. The roads leading to the colonia ran along the slightly raised ridges of glacial moraine. By the side of these roads close to the city walls were cemeteries where soldiers and civilians were buried. There it was the custom to set up elaborate memorials. Often citizens and soldiers would provide sculptured tombstones for themselves while still living as though it were a comforting thought to know that future generations would be able to read about their lives and careers.

When Julia Velva died, Aurelius Mercurialis her son, had a fine stone erected, which he had commissioned during his lifetime for his mother and his family. It shows Julia Velva at a funeral feast resting on a cushion on her couch. She holds a wine jar and her son stands at her side, a scroll, perhaps her will, in his hand. Seated below is a young girl, her daughter-in-law, holding a pet bird. Close by a young boy servant stands holding a wine jar in his left hand. His right hand rests on a small three-legged table. The inscription tells us that Julia Velva lived fifty years and was a dutiful mother. It is a rather touching little scene of family life.

One cannot but feel some sympathy for Caeresius Augustinius, a veteran of the Sixth Legion who dedicated an altar stone to his dear wife Flavia. She lived thirty-nine years, seven months, eleven days, but her son Augustus lived only one year, three days, while another child whose name we cannot read, lived only one year, nine months and five days.

A Roman Gravestone

Infant mortality in York was high. The alter stone shows Caeresius and Flavia and their two children, although strangely the boys are shown much older than their ages at death. It cannot therefore be a true likeness of them.

In Roman Britain people were subject to epidemics we can now control. They must have found the dampness and the winter mists of the Ouse Valley very troublesome and they doubtless suffered from rheumatism and chest complaints. Poor Luccius Duccius Ruffinus, the standard bearer to one of the maniples of the Ninth Legion was only twenty eight years old when he died. There were many like him who did not live to claim their honourable retirement and pension.

# RELIGION IN ROMAN YORK

Worship of the Emperor was the duty of all military and civil government officials. At the same time other gods could be worshipped and many religions were practised in York.

Besides the ancient gods of Greece and Rome, Roman soldiers worshipped the native gods of the places in which they served. As they moved on, some continued to worship these deities and to dedicate temples and altars to them. Such was the Egyptian God Seraphis to whom Claudius Hieronimianus, Imperial Legate and Commander of the Sixth Legion, built a temple in York completely 'from the ground upwards.'

Soldiers from the eastern fringe of the Empire and eastern merchants brought the Mithraic cult from Persia. They believed that in a dark cave Mithras slew the primordial bull, thereby bringing light and life to the earth, and by this act frustrated the forces of evil. Mithraism was a religion for men only. Its followers worshipped in small dark temples in an atmosphere made pungent by the scent of smouldering pine cones. They ate ritual meals and were admitted to the various degrees of their cult on completion of certain ordeals of purification. A sculptured relief showing Mithras slaying the bull has been found in York indicating that there was a temple there.

# CHRISTIAN WORSHIP

By contrast there has been very little found to indicate Christian worship. We know that Christianity was well established in Britain before the middle of the third century A.D. and that a Bishop from York was present at the Council of Arles in 3l4 A.D. Perhaps the Christian Church was on the site of St. Mary's Church, Bishop Hill. There is an apsidal building of Roman origin under this church. The Saxon tower of the present church also contains Roman masonry, but as yet no inscription or small find has been discovered to prove Christian origin. It would not be fair to assume however that Christianity was a religion of little importance because we cannot at present find small objects connected with Christian worship. Christianity in those days did not demand the manufacture of images or cult objects. Christians certainly worshipped in the Colonia at York and one day we may know where their church was built.

# LOCAL GODS

We find many inscriptions to other gods worshipped in York. Some of these inscriptions tell us a little about the people who paid their respects to these gods. Nikodemes, an Imperial Freedman visiting York on official business, gave thanks for his safe journey by setting up a statue and dedication to Britannia. Caius Julius Crescens worshipped the Matres, a popular trio of Celtic mother goddesses whose particular care was the home. Primulus set up an altar to Veteris, a Celtic god worshipped mainly by the poorer folk. Vitalis, a centurion, fulfilled his vow to Ariaco, another local god. Others wishing to play safe, preferred the more general dedication 'Deo Genio Loci,' to the god of this place - whoever he is! Marcus Minicius Mudenus, however, soldier of the Sixth Legion and river pilot, continued to put his trust in 'the mother goddesses of Africa, Italy and Gaul,' who had served him so well in the past.

# ANCIENT CLASSICAL GODS

Some were true to their old Gods. Publius Aelius Marcianus, prefect of an auxiliary cohort, pleased that his own health and that of his family had been preserved, hallowed and dedicated an altar to Jupiter 'best and greatest' and 'to the gods and goddesses of hospitality.' Agrius Auspex dedicated his altar to Mars the God of War and Sosia Iuncina wife of Quintus Antonius Isauricus, Commander in his time of the Sixth Legion, chose the goddess Fortune to honour the dedication of a double suite of baths, one for men and the other for women.

Silvanus, the god of the woods and the outdoors had his followers. Luccius Celerinius Vitalis, a clerk in the Ninth Legion dedicated an altar to him. There was also a temple of Hercules restored by Titus Publius Aeternus and a committee of priests and citizens of the same persuasion.

Religion was a powerful influence in Roman York. Its observances must have brought joy and comfort to citizens and soldiers alike, for many altars, dedication stones and small statues and cult objects have been discovered.

# HOME LIFE

Compared with anything which had gone before and with anything to be built for many centuries after the departure of the Romans, their homes were comfortable. Many were heated by hypocaust. The larger houses were arranged round a courtyard enclosing a pool or fountain. They had separate rooms for sleeping, eating and taking their leisure. Their furniture was simple, comfortable and elegantly decorated. Many households had slaves to do the hard work, leaving the lady of the house free to care for her own appearance or to teach the daughters of the family. Boys were more likely to study in small schools, each looked after by a master or an educated slave. They wrote their exercises on wax tablets with a stilus, or they scratched away with quill pen on papyrus, preparing themselves for careers in the army or the civil government.

## BEAUTY CARE AND FASHION

Roman ladies dyed their hair and used hair pieces. They often dressed it in elaborate fashion with fine beaded hairpins of Whitby jet. They used perfume. They made their faces up with cosmetics blended on small slate palettes and they studied the desired effect with hand mirrors of polished bronze. Young girls wore tunics and soft leather sandals. Their mothers would have more elaborate gowns or 'stolas.' These they would secure with brooches or clips fashioned in the shape of horses, cockerels, dragons or other animals. Such jewellery was often of Celtic design. To cool themselves, perhaps after an evening dinner party, they would use ivory fans. They wore necklaces and bangles made of beads of coral and jet and their rings were sometimes decorated with coloured cameos set in gold.

## DOMESTIC UTENSILS AND TABLEWARE

Cooking was done by slaves. Kitchen ware was of beaten and riveted bronze. In poorer homes,where bronze utensils would have been too costly, earthenware pots were used. The ordinary folk had dishes, bowls and drinking beakers of Castor ware, a dark pottery coming from the valley of the river Nene and often decorated with native design in creamy colours showing hares, dogs and other animals. The rich preferred to impress their friends with fine Samian table-ware imported from Gaul. This was brownish-orange in colour, glazed and with decoration in relief. Their dining tables were lit by flickering oil lamps hung in elegant lamp standards and they lounged on couches and gossiped between the courses.

# THE SHOPS

In the small open-fronted shops round the forum, meat and other commodities were weighed with small hanging scales of bronze or with bronze steelyards with a sliding weight and graduated bar. Merchants and traders, when the hours of business were over, packed-up their stock and secured their premises with locks and padlocks very similar to those we use today. Business transactions were sometimes noted on wax tablets and the choppers and knives used by the butcher were very similar to those used today.

# ENTERTAINMENTS

Some towns had a theatre for plays and an arena for 'circus games' as gladiator sports were called. We do not really know whether York had either of these, but at least one gladiator's lucky bronze charm has been found bearing the inscription 'Domine Victor, Vincas Felix' or Champion may you have a lucky win. We must hope that this charm was effective and that its owner lived perhaps to fight again another day.

We can be reasonably sure that a good deal of tippling went on. Large amphorae, in which wine was stored, have been turned-up and perhaps it was a happy centurion who once possessed the fine drinking mug in Castor ware, now in the Yorkshire Museum, bearing the inscription 'Nolite Sitire' - don't get thirsty.

There must have been many inns or canteens in the colonia. One had a handsome mosaic floor showing the god Bacchus. Some time ago the discovery in a cemetery of a young lady's skeleton with very well articulated vertebrae, but with a broken thigh-bone, caused some speculation. Could she have been an entertainer, an acrobatic dancer perhaps, who slipped on wine spilled on this very floor and broke her leg? We shall never know. Whatever her talents they did not bring wealth for she was buried simply among poor people.

# DISTINGUISHED VISITORS AND CITIZENS OF YORK

The colonia at York saw many important personalities besides those citizens who lived normal undistinguished lives. No fewer than three Emperors of Rome visited the Colonia each with splendid retinue. The Emperor Severus and his son Caracalla made York their base when they campaigned against the Scottish tribes from 208 to 211 A.D. The Roman Empire was governed from York during this time. There is fragmentary archaeological evidence to suggest that an imposing colonnaded palace, probably built for Severus, once occupied a site by the riverside where the church of All Saints' North Street now stands, and there are the remains of a large bath house nearby. Severus died in York in 211 A.D. never having performed the sacrifice of thanks-giving to the God of War for his victories. Rumour has it that the sacrificial animals provided for the ceremony were black instead of white and that the Emperor left the temple in disgust. Careless attendants allowed the black animals to follow him to his palace. This was not a good omen because the Emperor died shortly afterwards and was cremated with great ceremony in York.

The visit of the Emperor Constantius Chlorus to York during the usurpation of Carausius and Allectus in Britain, and the improvements he made to the defences of the fortress have been described earlier in this book. He too died in York and his son Constantine, who had ridden in fourteen days along the imperial highway from Rome to be at his father's bedside, was proclaimed Emperor in York.

Reference to lesser persons connected with York sometimes comes to light in distant places. Marcus Aurelius Lunaris, the York priest, set up his altar at Bordeaux and thereby gave us precise information of the town's status as a Colonia. Publius Mumminius Sissenna Rutilianus is another Roman, part of whose life was connected with the place. He commenced his career in the Imperial service as a junior officer with the Fifth Legion in Austria. Later he held the posts of Quaestor, Tribune and Praetor in the civil service and then, as a Legate, he commanded the Sixth Legion in York. After this he was appointed Consul and Governor of Upper Moesia and he completed his career as Proconsul in Asia. On retirement he was patron of his birth place, Tibur near Rome, and it is from an inscription in his honour there that we learn of his service in York. There must have been many other dignitaries and officials of the Empire who had served a tour in North Britain and perhaps like Publius in the Colonia at York.

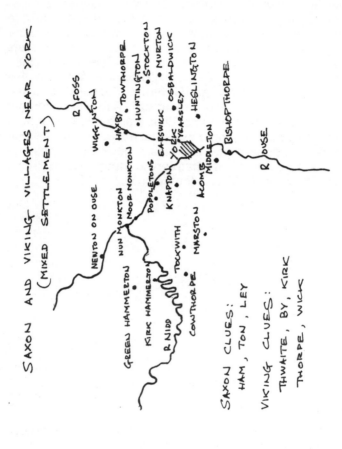

SAXON AND VIKING VILLAGES NEAR YORK
(MIXED SETTLEMENT)

R. FOSS

R. OUSE

R. NIDD

NEWTON ON OUSE

GREEN HAMMERTON

KIRK HAMMERTON

COWTHORPE

TOCKWITH

NUN MONKTON

MOOR MONKTON

POPPLETONS

MARSTON

KNAPTON

ACOMB

MIDDLETON

YORK

WIGGINTON

HAXBY

TOWTHORPE

HUNTINGTON

STOCKTON

EARSWICK

MURTON

OSBALDWICK

YEARSLEY

HESLINGTON

BISHOPTHORPE

SAXON CLUES:
HAM, TON, LEY

VIKING CLUES:
THWAITE, BY, KIRK
THORPE, WICK

38

# Chapter Four

# ANGLIAN YORKSHIRE

The period between 400 A.D. and 1066 A.D. was the most formative period in our history. This was the time during which Saxon and Scandinavian folk settled in the country. It was the period when our language, our laws, our church, our system of government, our place names, our weights and measures, our coinage and many of our territorial boundaries were established. How did all this come about?

# THE SAXON INVASIONS

By the late fourth century the power of Rome was declining under the pressure of invasions from without and ineptitude and corruption within. All round the fringes of the Empire barbarian peoples were raiding the provinces seeking advantage for themselves. Britain, the most distant of all the provinces, came under attack by Jutes, Angles and Saxons from across the North Sea. Elaborate coastal defences, forts, watch towers and a fleet failed to keep these raiders at bay. When the defence of Rome itself made necessary the final withdrawal of the legions in 410 A.D., local Romano British leaders tried to resist, or made use of mercenary soldiers or 'foederati' from among the invaders themselves to protect them from further raids, but all was in vain. Pirates,who had come at first for plunder,now came to stay and to establish themselves on land easier to work than that which they had farmed in their homelands in the Frisian swamps and on the Danish Peninsula and the North German Plain.

The invaders were sturdy self-reliant stock. They were good farmers and fishermen accustomed alike to hard work and to the dangers of the open sea,where they hunted seals and whales. They made the crossing to Britain in open boats, clinker-built of oak, each one about seventy feet long and eleven feet wide, their overlapping planks clenched with iron nails. With fourteen oars on each side they could easily elude the clumsy Roman Galleys and penetrate the river valleys of the east coast. In this way they entered the Vale of York by Humber and Ouse. Each boat carried forty invaders, the menfolk armed with eight foot iron spears shafted with ash, iron swords, bows and iron tipped arrows.

The Saxons had a social organisation based on mutual respect and loyalty, each boatload of free men obeying and following their thegn. Danger and cold nights at sea had taugh them the advantages of co-operation which made them first rate pioneers. They saw the vast extent of virgin land in Britain and in the next two hundred years they spread over the country, clearing the forests, draining the meadows cutting into the more difficult clay soils with their heavy iron tipped wheeled ploughs and establishing countless villages, hamlets, tons and burghs. The system of agriculture they established was to last in many parts until the enclosures and improvements of the l8th century and the profile of their fields can sometimes still be seen today in the ridges and furrows on the land.

The economy of a Saxon village was based on the crops taken from three large communally-held fields. These fields were divided into strips a furrow-long from which our measure furlong comes. At first all cleared land was 'folk land' and belonged to the community. The strips in the fields were allocated according to the needs of each family. As time went on holdings differed in size until the thegns,or local leaders in society,might hold as much as five hides or six hundred acres, whereas the holdings of a 'gebur' or peasant would perhaps average thirty acres and 'cottars' or cottagers would hold less still. Serfs or bondsmen 'thralls' or 'theows' would hold no land at all and be much like slaves working as haywards, oxherds, ploughmen, beekeepers, swineherds, shepherds or woodwards. A freeman could be reduced to this plight by capture in war, by enemy raids or by failure of crops causing him to sell his family into bondage.

The crops grown on two of the fields were winter-sown wheat and spring barley. The third field was left fallow to regain its fertility. This system gave a simple three year rotation and ensured that the fallow field would be manured by cattle folded to graze on whatever might grow in the fallow year. It lacked a root crop, which would have given a much better balance and would have enabled the farmers to control the weeds, but it was better than any system that had gone before. Heavier soils were being brought into cultivation and the thick forests of the broad Yorkshire vales were being cleared. A hay-crop was lifted from the water-meadows or 'ings' in early summer. Cattle were pastured on the commons and pigs were driven to root in the forests surrounding the villages, turning-up acorns, beech nuts and saplings and making the work of clearing the forests for new fields easier. The Saxons varied their diet with game and fish which abounded; they ate fruit in season and they were great drinkers of ale and mead. The words 'ham' for hamlet, 'ton' for town or settlement, 'ley' and 'mede' for pasture occurring in place-names all over the best arable land of Yorkshire today give ample evidence of original Saxon settlement.

# ADMINISTRATION AND THE LAW

Disputes were settled locally as far as possible. For from the age of twelve upwards each man had to belong to a 'tithing' or group of ten. All ten were pledged to ensure the good behaviour of the others in the group. Matters were discussed by all the free men of the hamlet in the 'Folk Moot' under the thegn. More weighty questions could be decided at the 'Hundred Moot.' The Shire Reve or King's official presided at the 'Shire Moot' and the 'Witan Moot', or highest council in the land, existed to advise the King on important matters of defence, law and justice concerning the whole kingdom.

Trial for crimes was often by ordeal and the punishment for offences was by an agreed system of fines or 'wergeld' which provided compensation for the injured party. The 'wer-geld' for the death of a thegn could be as high as 6000 silver shillings and that for a gebur upwards of 800 shillings. There were lesser sums, perhaps payable in copper coins for lesser injuries. There was a certain amount of money in circulation. Silver scaettas were first minted in Northumbria by King

Eadbert 737-759 A.D. and copper stycas by King Osrea 781-790 A.D. The Archbishop of York also had the right to mint coins up to 876 A.D. Besides these there were many other coins in circulation mostly of foreign origin. The death penalty was rare and only for crimes such as treason, arson and witchcraft.

# THE SEVEN SAXON KINGDOMS

Saxon kingdoms were soon established. The basis was loyalty of thegn and freeman alike to their king. The Angles, who settled in Yorkshire were governed by Aella and their Kingdom Deira had boundaries similar to those of the county today. Later, after a great deal of fighting with the native population, this kingdom was extended to the north to the Firth of Forth and to the west to the Cumbrian Coast. Northumbria was the kingdom of all the peoples living north of the Humber. There were by then seven kingdoms in Britain: Northumbria, Mercia, East Anglia, Middlesex, Kent, Sussex and Wessex.

# RELIGION IN NORTHUMBRIA

The Saxons were originally pagans worshipping the old Norse gods of the elements. There was Tiw the god of the sky or sun, Odin the god of wisdom and of war, Thor the god of lightning and the storm and protector of the peasant and Freyja the fertility goddess. The Saxon invasions drove the Romano-British Christians far westwards to Wales and Ireland,where the Celtic Christian Church remained cut off from Western Christendom for almost a hundred and fifty years.

The Christian faith was brought back to Kent in 597 A.D. by St. Augustine and his fellow Benedictine Monks. There, favourable circumstances caused by the marriage of the Jutish King Ethelbert to Bertha, the Christian daughter of the King of Paris, made it possible for the Pope to send a mission to the Kentish Court which proved successful. In a similar way, the marriage of King Edwin of Northumbria in 625 A.D. to Ethelburga, Christian daughter of this earlier Kentish royal marriage,brought Paulinus to York as chaplain to the bride and as a missionary to the Northumbrian Court. In 626 A.D. Paulinus became the first Bishop of York and on Easter Day

627, King Edwin was himself baptised at a holy well situated under the font in the present Minster. The first timber church was hastily erected for this occasion. The conversion of Edwin had not been easily accomplished, for he had demanded guarantees for dissolving his allegiance to the gods of his forefathers. A curious train of circumstances seemed to give those guarantees. He saw a vision promising him greatness, he had success in battle against his west Saxon enemies and he was delivered from an assassination plot on the very day his baby daughter was born. He in turn persuaded many of his councillors and advisers to be baptised with him. But before the celebration his official party, led by Coefi the high priest of the old religion, rode out to the Pagan Temple at Goodmanham near Market Weighton and, to the astonishment of the locals, officially desecrated and burned the wooden structure.

Baptism of Edwin

The early success of the Christians in Northumbria was short-lived for Edwin was killed by the heathen Mercians. Paulinus fled with Ethelburga back to Kent and missionary work was left to the intrepid James the Deacon, who continued undaunted preaching in the countryside round Leyburn and Catterick. Elsewhere most of the early converts no doubt reverted to their former pagan beliefs.

It was not until Oswald, son of Ethelfrid, who had preceeded Edwin as King, had secured the Northumbrian Kingdom in 634 A.D. that the patient work of conversion could continue. Oswald had been taught by Celtic Christian monks in the tiny colony established on Iona by St. Columba, who had crossed the sea from Ireland to this lovely island off the west coast of Scotland. Oswald invited St. Aidan to bring some monks from Iona to found a missionary centre at Lindisfarne, the 'Holy Island' close by his royal stronghold at Bamborough and to conduct missions within his Kingdom. This enterprise proved successful much further afield than in Northumbria. Diuma took the gospel to the Mercians, St. Cedd became the first Bishop of Essex, St. Wilfrid converted Sussex and at home St. Chad became Bishop of York. It was the period of the early preaching crosses, of which there are many examples in Yorkshire. That at Easby near Richmond is well known and tells in simple relief in stone much of the Christian story. The example at Holy Trinity Stonegrave near Ampleforth is simpler in form, decorated with the characteristic strap-work carving of the period and showing the evangelist with a book, the Cross of Christ and Christ himself ascending in majesty. Each cross or preaching centre took the name monasterium or monastery, recognised today in the term minster applied to churches with early Saxon foundation. The Celtic monks lived together simply in single cells grouped in a monastery and surrounding a church. After a period of recuperation and inspiration they moved out, preaching in the open air at the stone crosses up and down the land, for village churches had not yet been built.

# SAXON CHRISTIANITY.

CELTIC MISSION

TO PICTS AND SCOTS

ST COLUMBA SAILED TO IONA CELTIC MISSION

ST AIDAN BUILT THE CELTIC MISSION ON LINDISFARNE

IRELAND

RIPON

YORK

SYNOD OF WHITBY 664 AD

CONFUSION IN TEACHING

ST AUGUSTINE'S MISSION
CANTERBURY

TWO SEPARATE MISSIONS BROUGHT THE GOSPEL TO YORKSHIRE

THE MISSION OF PAULINUS AND LATER WILFRID REPRESENTED ST AUGUSTINE'S MISSION FROM ROME.

ST AIDAN AND HIS FOLLOWERS REPRESENTED THE OLD CELTIC TRADITION FROM IRELAND AND IONA. DIFFERENCES OF OPINION WERE SETTLED AT WHITBY BY KING OSWY OF NORTHUMBRIA.

# THE SYNOD OF WHITBY

By the seventh century there was a divergence of missionary effort. The Benedictine monks from Rome had continued their work in the southern kingdoms, when all had seemed lost during the troubled times in the north following Edwin's death. Now, under royal patronage, the north was being evangelised by missionaries of the Celtic Church. There were basic differences of doctrine and in the way in which the church was to be organised which, if unresolved, would hinder missionary effort. The two missions were not in agreement over the timing of Easter and the great Christian festivals. Benedictine monks favoured the tonsure, the method of shaving the head of a priest in remembrance of the crowning of our Lord with the crown of thorns, the Celtic monks did not. The Celtic monks lived in the more primitive tradition of the early Christian hermits, whereas Roman monks led a

Synod of Whitby

corporate life governed by the Rule of St. Benedict. Moreover, in the Celtic Church bishops were still part of the monastic community and the territory for which they were responsible was not clearly laid down. The Roman church favoured bishops living the life of secular clergy and each responsible for a properly defined bishopric.

Domestic affairs at court were again the moving force. King Oswy, Oswald's successor, a Christian of the Celtic persuasion, found it impossible to celebrate the joyous feast of Easter, while his Queen, a Christian of the Roman Church, was still enduring the solemn privations of Lent. Consequently a Synod was convened at Whitby in 664 A.D. in the monastery presided over by St. Hilda, an abbess and princess of the Northumbrian Royal House. Oswy listened to the case of the Celtic Christians ably put by Bishop Colman and St. Cedd and to the case of the Romans argued by St. Wilfrid and the Venerable James the Deacon. St. Wilfrid had travelled widely and had visited Rome and had audience with the Pope. He could see the advantage of the more highly organised administration of the Roman Church. The Roman mission claimed to be the true representatives of St. Peter,holder of the Keys to Heaven. The Celtic monks could make no such claim and acceded humbly to the King's decision in favour of the Roman mission. Henceforth the die was set for undivided missionary effort and for the beginning of a golden age of Christian scholarship in Northumbria. Bede, the great scholar of Jarrow, was soon to write the 'History of the English Church and People' and Alcuin was to make the library at York the finest centre of Christian learning in northern Europe.

# TOWN LIFE

Not much is known of town life in early Saxon times. The Saxons were not town dwellers, though as pirates and traders they appreciated the work of town craftsmen. There were Romano-British towns in Yorkshire of which the Colonia of York was the greatest. No doubt life continued here as long as possible but as things grew worse the citizens were either killed or they ran away and the fine buildings fell into ruins. In

York archaeological evidence suggests that defensive ditches silted-up and there was extensive flooding between 450 and 500 A.D. making the place almost impossible to live in. There are only isolated examples of Saxon buildings built directly on Roman footings. If there had been more it might have proved continuous occupation. Moreover, the Saxon kings themselves lived a wandering life with their courts and this was scarcely likely to lead to the establishment of even one capital town.

By the beginning of the seventh century however, York had begun again to assume some importance. It was here that Paulinus came with Ethelburga to Edwin's court. Pope Gregory had given instructions to Augustine in Canterbury, that if the mission to Northumbria succeeded, he was to appoint twelve bishops to assist Paulinus, who was to enjoy the 'metropolitan dignity.' Paulinus found little remaining of the flourishing Roman city. If there had been even the remains of a stone church he would no doubt have had it repaired as Augustine had done in Canterbury. We know however, that it was necessary to build a temporary wooden minster for Edwin's baptism and work on the permanent church went on for six or seven years more. This work would scarcely have taken so long if there had been a flourishing town there. Even in 664 A.D., when the great decision was made to follow the teachings of the Roman Church, the synod did not take place at York, but at Whitby. There may have been no proper religious life in York at this time for,when Wilfrid came to re-establish the dicocese, he found the church of St. Peter in a very poor way. The roof was leaking, there were no coverings for the windows and the inside was soiled by bird droppings. It was his re-establishment of the see of York however and of the school there,which was to lead to a gradual increase in the importance of the city late in Saxon times. A much more rapid expansion came in Viking times when York became an important trading port in the Scandinavian empire.

# THE COPPERGATE HELMET

Who was Oshere? We do not know. Was he a warrior of noble or kingly estate? Was he a merchant, a man of wealth who could afford to commission such a splendid helmet for a gift to a warrior? Was he a metalsmith, the maker of the helmet? The name Oshere in Saxon times is not uncommon but we have no written evidence to fall back upon to explain the origins or ownership of this remarkable piece. How then was Oshere's helmet lost and when was it found?

Oshere's helmet was found almost by accident by two construction workers during the redevelopment of Coppergate in York in May 1982 after the official Coppergate Dig had been completed. It is a helmet of Saxon craftsmanship bearing some similarity to the celebrated Sutton Hoo Helmet,buried in 625 A.D. with great ceremony at Sutton Hoo in Suffolk in a boat with the grave goods and treasures of a great king,probably Raedwald.But unlike the Sutton Hoo Helmet Oshere's helmet was buried in a rubbish pit or a well in Anglian York. When it was found there were some wooden remains of the lining of the pit surrounding it. There was an iron spearhead nearby. There was a piece of antler, some metal worker's slag and one or two unidentifiable wooden articles and twigs which may have fallen in afterwards. The helmet appeared to have been carefully placed with its chain mail neck protection and hinged cheek pieces neatly packed and folded inside. Was it therefore intended that it might be recovered after some danger had passed? The helmet was most probably old and much used when it was abandoned in the pit. Perhaps Oshere was already dead. Any conclusions we may wish to make at present will be guesswork.

The helmet is made from iron plates riveted together and strengthened with decorative brass bands. One long plate encircles the head with semi-circular openings below the brow to make eyepieces. Two other plates cross from front to back and from side to side forming the basis of the dome of the helmet and the four triangular spaces between are filled with further plates of iron. The whole,during construction and possibly during the riveting process,was beaten to a fine

natural rounded shape to enclose the warrior's head. Inside
would have been leather or felt packing to cushion any blow.
The sides of the helmet once bore two hinged cheek pieces
one of which still remains. The nape of the warrior's neck was
protected by intricately woven chain mail, secured to the back
of the helmet and to the cheek pieces and now, like the rest of
the helmet, carefully restored. A finely wrought brass
noseguard completes the helmet.

The Coppergate Helmet

The materials used to make the helmet are not so costly as
those used for the Sutton Hoo burial helmet. There is no gold
or silver wire in its construction and no garnets or precious
stones decorate it. But the helmet is no less significant for that.
It is a helmet made for use and not simply for ceremonial and
parade. Its style and craftsmanship are indisputably
Northumbrian and equal in sophistication to that of Sutton Hoo

which incidentally may even be of Swedish origin and not English. When the helmet of Oshere was made, possibly in York, its construction in less costly materials may suggest that precious metals were beyond the reach of the Northumbrian nobility at that time, but the standard of craftsmanship evident in its making is superb as one would expect.

The brass straps which decorate and strengthen the helmet give the best clues to suggest dating the helmet. The strap which passes from front to back holds in position a plate with an inscription in Latin which is Christian and which is probably a prayer intended to invoke the help and protection of God in battle. It is translated into English as, 'In the name of our Lord Jesus, the Holy Spirit, God the Father and with all we pray. Amen, Oshere.' The letters are raised and for extra effect the prayer is repeated on the straps which pass from side to side across the top of the helmet. But here on the right hand side, the writing is reversed as though the metalsmith who made the helmet was following the directions of a scribe, though only partly understanding the form of the letters. The helmet was therefore not made before the arrival of St. Paulinus to York in 626 A.D. The shape of the letters of the inscription and the curious nature of the animal head decoration on the brass strapwork of the helmet tend to suggest that it was made in the late seventh or early eighth century because this same form of decoration illuminates the Lindisfarne Gospels. The intertwined animal decoration on the nose piece is however typical of a more limited period of time between 750 and 775 A.D. and this is most probably when the helmet was made.

When the helmet was lost it was already damaged most likely in battle. It was old because the brasswork showed signs of wear from constant cleaning just as the brass cap badges proudly shown by old soldiers to new recruits today have a smoothness about them that can only be achieved by years of polishing with metal polish and brush.

Could it be possible that the helmet of Oshere was lost or hidden when the Vikings invaded York in 866 A.D.? Whatever its origin or fate its rediscovery brings back to us a great Northumbrian treasure.

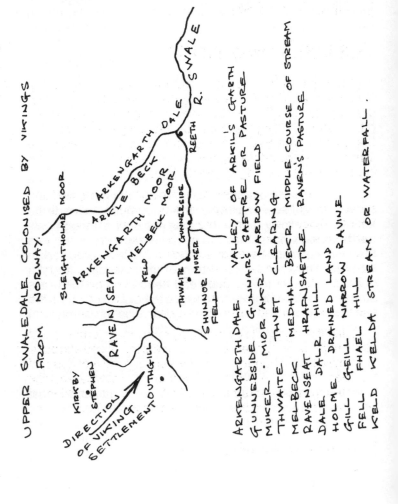

UPPER SWALEDALE COLONISED BY VIKINGS FROM NORWAY.

DIRECTION OF VIKING SETTLEMENT

KIRKBY STEPHEN

SLEIGHTHOLME MOOR

ARKENGARTH DALE
ARKLE BECK
ARKENGARTH MOOR
MELBECK MOOR
REETH
GUNNERSIDE
R. SWALE

RAVEN SEAT
KELD
THWAITE
MUKER
SHUNNOR FELL

ARKENGARTH DALE — VALLEY OF ARKIL'S GARTH
GUNNERSIDE — GUNNAR'S SAETRE OR PASTURE
MUKER — MIOR AKR NARROW FIELD
THWAITE — THVET CLEARING
MELBECK — MEDHAL BECK MIDDLE COURSE OF STREAM
RAVENSEAT — HRAFNSAETRE RAVEN'S PASTURE
DALR — DALR HILL
HOLME — DRAINED LAND
GILL — GEILL NARROW RAVINE
FELL — FHAEL HILL
KELD — KELDA STREAM OR WATERFALL.

# Chapter Five

# VIKING YORKSHIRE

## THE VIKING INVASIONS

At the end of the eighth century the Saxon kingdom of Northumbria suffered a severe setback. In 793 A.D. the first band of Viking marauders burned and sacked the monastery of Lindisfarne, killing the monks and stealing their treasures. Soon afterwards Bede's monastery at Jarrow suffered the same fate. As the attacks continued it seemed that the whole country would be plunged into darkness and terror.

Who were these pagans who arrived on the wind, wild and savage as gulls? The people of Northumbria called them Vikings. They were men of the Scandinavian fjords and the sandy creeks of Denmark. For them life was hard. Land was scarce and piracy offered adventure and a chance of wealth. During the next two centuries they were to colonise the north of Britain, Iceland, Greenland and even the coast of North America. To the east they penetrated the heartland of Russia and their ships sailed on the Black Sea to threaten Byzantium.

At first the longboats came singly or in small numbers, but as the raids gained impetus their numbers increased and once as many as three hundred and fifty were seen at the mouth of the Thames. In 865 A.D. the host, as they were now called, took to wintering in East Anglia and in 867 A.D. under their chieftain Ivar, they landed from the Humber and captured York.

## THE VIKING KINGDOM

The Saxon kingdom soon collapsed. Archbishop Wulfere took refuge temporarily in Mercia and the north was ruled from 876 A.D. to 954 A.D. by a succession of Viking kings: Halfdan, Guthred, Siefred, Cnut, Regnald, Guthfrith, Sithric, Eric Bloodaxe and others, for several met sudden and violent ends.

Guthred, who was elected on the death of Halfdan in 880 A.D. was the first ChristianViking king in York, and there was comparative peace in his reign as many of his followers abandoned their pagan beliefs and followed his example.

The struggle of the Saxon kingdoms of the south to re-establish supremacy over the north is long. King Alfred of Wessex came to terms with the Vikings in Mercia and the south. For eighteen years his children Edward and Aethelflaed sought a lasting treaty with the north. Athelstan established a common coinage throughout all the land and in conciliation gave his sister in marriage to Sithric, Viking king of York, but the Viking settlers of York preferred their own King to a Saxon. When Eric Bloodaxe finally lost the northern kingdom to the Saxons in 954 A.D. no more Viking Kings were elected and Saxon earls kept a strong hold on the land for more than a hundred years until the Norman conquest. Nor was any Northumbrian appointed to the Archbishopric of York, for in the difficult days after 947 A.D. even Archbishop Wulfstan, having pledged himself to Eadred the Saxon king, had betrayed his trust. To pay for this, Ripon, the only great northern monastery to have escaped the earlier raids was sacked.

# VIKING SETTLEMENT

Penetration of the north by Viking settlers had commenced soon after the raids and had taken two forms. Settlers from Denmark colonised the Plain of Holderness and the Vale of York, where there was land to spare in the forest and waste between Saxon settlements. Vikings from Norway sailed round the north coast of Scotland colonising the Western Isles, Ireland, the Isle of Man and the west coast of Northumbria. From there they moved inland into the Pennine Dales to lands similar, though a great deal less hostile to farming effort than their homeland.

# PLACE-NAME EVIDENCE

Saxon village names often contain descriptive words: 'ham' for hamlet, 'ton' for village, 'ley' for pasture, 'stead, fold' or 'stoke' for enclosure, 'holt' for health or 'dean' for clearing. Similarly

Viking settlements are recognisable, their place-names giving some indications of original land use. 'Thwaite' indicates a clearing, 'saetr' means high pasture, 'wick' a granary, 'holme' a stretch of well drained land, 'gill' a narrow ravine and 'fell' a hill, 'by' or 'byth' a byre and 'beck' a stream, while 'kirk' indicates the existence of a church.

# MIXED SETTLEMENT ON THE PLAINS

Throughout the Plain of Holderness and in the Vale of York, particularly round the city of York, Saxon and Viking settlements existed side by side. The Viking freemen mixed fairly easily with their Saxon neighbours marrying Saxon girls and eventually producing a fairly well integrated society. There were many areas of similarity. Both peoples had originally worshipped the same pagan gods and were now alike converted to Christianity. Both peoples came from similar tribal backgrounds and now had the same respect for the law, for from the reign of Edgar 959-975 A.D., the two peoples were equal in the eyes of that law. The Saxon 'Moot' was similar to the Viking assembly of freemen the 'Thing' and the Saxon 'Hundred' approximated to the Viking 'Wappentake.' As well as this, where geographical conditions were similar, Saxon and Viking farming methods were the same and so there was no conflict of interests in this respect.

# VIKING SETTLEMENT IN THE DALES

A different pattern of settlement however is to be seen towards the head of the Pennine Dales, where Vikings from Norway entered Yorkshire from the west. Here there were few Saxon settlements and here the land favoured a type of farming similar to that of the Scandinavian homelands. Transhumance was practised. Cattle pastured on the high moors in the good summer weather would be brought down to valley bottoms in the winter and breeding stock would be fed on hay harvested from the bottom meadows during the previous summer. The upper courses of Swaledale show this most clearly, for here present day place names are still largely those of the original Viking settlers. Arkengarthdale is the valley of Arkil's garth or enclosure. Ravenseat is Raefen's saetr or pasture. Gunnerside is Gundar's pasture. The village of Muker was built by a mior-akr or narrow field. Keld was by a stream or kelda, Oxnop was oxa-hop or oxen valley and Melbecks was medhalbekkr or the middle course of the stream. Close by are Sleightholme moor, Outhgill, Shunnor Fell and other Viking names. The upper Pennine Dales were widely colonised by the Scandinavians.

St. Gregory's Minster, Kirkdale

# AN ANGLO-VIKING MINSTER

In Kirkdale in a narrow limestone valley beneath the wide expanse of the North York Moors and close by a beck St. Gregory's Minster lies far from the nearest houses. 'Orm, Gamal's son bought St. Gregory's Minster when it was all broken down and fallen and he let it be made anew from the ground to Christ and St. Gregory, in Edward's days, the king, and in Tosti's days, the Earl,' reads the dedication on the wide sundial now positioned over the doorway. How did this remarkably well authenticated church come to occupy this position and what story does this dedication stone tell?

The church is pre-conquest. Stone slabs discovered on the site and now safely kept in the Chancel once bore the inscription 'Cyning Aethilwild.' Could this be the site of the monastery founded by St. Cedd in the 7th Century?

In his history Bede tells us that Aethilwild, son of King Oswald, desired St. Cedd to accept some land to found a monastery, to which the king himself might go to offer prayers and hear the gospel and where he might be buried when the time came. If this is so St. Cedd chose in Kirkdale a craggy and desolate spot for his cell, but a place of great natural beauty. We are told that the saint planned to spend all of Lent there in prayer to cleanse the place of possible former unholy associations. He was called away on royal affairs, but his place was taken by his brother Cynebil, who built the first monastery and established the Celtic custom of Lindisfarne.

This being so the dedication to St. Gregory is interesting. There had been a certain disagreement between the Celtic monks and the mission from Rome led at St. Gregory's wish by St. Augustine in 597 A.D. However this disagreement had been solved in Northumbria at the Synod of Whitby in 664 A.D. St. Cedd, who had been at the Synod, agreed to the adoption of the Roman rite and the dedication of the new foundation to St. Gregory, Bishop of Rome, may have been a deliberate attempt to foster Christian unity in the North.

The Minster had first been built in 654 A.D. or soon afterwards. It was destroyed during the Viking invasions and lay in ruins for many years until it was re-built in the reign of King Edward the Confessor, when Tostig, half brother of Harold Godwinson, was Earl of Northumbria.

Orm, the builder of the present Minster, was a wealthy local landowner. His father Gamal had been murdered by Tostig and doubtless this is one of the crimes for which Tostig was exiled to Norway in 1065 A.D. According to local legend Orm intended to build the church close to the hamlets of Nawton and Wombleton. The stone was assembled on the site, but the next morning, when work was about to commence, it was found to have been removed to the original site of St. Gregory's Minster. It was taken back again to the new site, but each time by night some mysterious agency returned it to the dale, so in the end it was felt better to re-erect the church on its original site where it stands today distant from the houses and a living monument to Anglo-Viking Christianity.

# JORVIK

Eboracum, Eoforwic, Jorvik, York. The pronunciation of the name of the city of York has changed from Roman times to the present day. York is the closest to the Scandinavian Jorvik, for J was soft in the nothern tongue.

The expansion of the small royal and ecclesiastical burgh of Anglian times into a flourishing trading centre, second only to London in population, and well linked into a Scandinavian sea empire is one of the most significant events in the history of this period. When Edward the Confessor reigned in London and Tostig was Earl in the North, there must have been over one thousand, seven hundred homes in the city, which was divided into separate wards or 'liberties.' In one 'liberty' the Archbishop had sole jurisdiction and profit, elsewhere the King and others derived considerable income from rents.

# ARCHAEOLOGICAL FINDS

Items found are local pottery, pottery from East Anglia and the south, pins, brooches, skates, beads, bodkins, bronze bowls, musical instruments, coins found singly and in hoards, a moneyer's die, amber beads, some polished and others as yet unfinished, a golden ring and a superb helmet. They give some indication of the items in use in Jorvik and of the commodities used in trade.

At Bishophill, close by the church, a remarkable fish processing plant with washing cisterns and drying racks has been unearthed. Here herrings by the thousand could be prepared for local markets or for trade further afield. Elsewhere, on land left almost unused in Saxon time, there is evidence from small finds of the spoils of many different workshops set up in the Viking period.

Some distance further away at the end of the Pavement in Coppergate and underneath Lloyds Bank and the York Coffee House, there are more signs of 9th century commercial undertakings. Here a number of buildings have recently been unearthed. The evidence is of large stone-supported posts, such as would provide the main joists of framed-up houses, with plaited or woven wicker-work walls plastered with clay, and with floors of brush wood bonded with beaten clay.

These were the workshop-homes of the leather workers and other craftsmen. There are shallow curing pits and wooden stretching frames, fragments of wooden eating bowls, worked antlers, bone combs of considerable artistic merit, and gold and silver-plated rings. The Viking craftsmen and merchants lived a prosperous enough life, but they lived in great squalor surrounded by rubbish, the debris of animals and fish, and in an atmosphere rank with the smell of rotting hides. Presumably the manufacturing and commercial area of the city extended over a wide area and must have presented an untidy but vigorous spectacle.

A number of grave slabs with animal headed interlaced decoration, hog-backed memorials and sculptured cross shafts found in the city also give some indication of the wealth of some citizens and of their desire to beautify its churches.

# THE COPPERGATE DIG

Further evidence of the extent and scope of the manufacturing and commercial activities of the Vikings in York has been confirmed by the more recent Coppergate dig conducted by the York Archaeological Trust between 1976 and 1981. Coppergate, named in Viking time as the street of the coopers, or barrel makers and woodturners is an inner city area between the rivers Ouse and Foss, where wet clay and black waterlogged soil have preserved four rows of long timber buildings, mainly of oak, running parallel to the street. So well has the wet soil preserved both large and small objects that it has been possible not only to see the homes, shops and workshops of the Vikings, but also the multitude of small objects which would otherwise have perished.

Among the metal objects found have been such necessary items as fish hooks, spoons, knives, some with handles complete, spurs and locks and keys. Among the less necessary metal items are plated brooches bangles and rings.

A great quantity of bone work has been found, some decorated with animals scratched into the surface in true to life form and some etched in the more stylised design favoured by Viking craftsmen and not unlike the interlocking curving and writhing designs favoured by the writers of the Lindisfarne Gospels. There were fragments of crucibles made of earthenware with residual glass coating the inner surfaces indicating that ornamental glass was manufactured and there were a number of glass beads to be threaded for necklaces. Quantities of amber were discovered, which must have been imported from the Baltic, and which were to be used for the manufacture of the beads and pendants traded in York from the jewellers' workshops. Combs, pins, spindles and buttons of bone were commonplace as were fragments of leatherwork and textiles, some locally woven, others imported from Arab lands. There were wooden spoons and cups and the waste plugs from the woodturners' lathes and there were dice carved from bone and walrus ivory.

A cowrie shell from the Red Sea or the Arabian Sea somehow found its way to Viking York and coins from distant Samarkand were in the hands of York merchants indicating the distance over which Viking merchants traded. English coins were also in evidence. Fine silver pennies, minted for King Edgar between 960 and 973 A.D., were found in a building thought to be a shop fronting on Coppergate, the principal street. Other evidence, this time of the moneyer's craft, was soon forthcoming. A number of lead strips thought to be the die maker's test pieces stamped with the face and reverse of coins were later discovered. One was an example of a St. Peters' Penny showing a sword and the hammer of Thor. Another was from the reign of King Athelstan 924-939 A.D., the Saxon king who united north and south after the defeat of the Viking kings. A third trial strip found shows the face of a coin of the Saxon

King Eadwig who ruled from 955 to 959 A.D. The moneyer who struck this coin was probably named Frothric for his name appears on the test strip. The letters of his name appear reversed as in a mirror image, a mistake that was not uncommon in those days when even the moneyer may have been illiterate. He worked from a design produced by a scribe and probably did not realise that the letters must be reversed in the die.

The discovery of trial pieces and dies is particularly fortunate since evidence of the moneyer's craft is rare in excavations. There being no centralised mint, York may have been the only die cutting and minting centre north of the Humber. It follows that, since only people of wealth and influence were entrusted to mint coins, merchants of this class must have been living and trading in Coppergate.

Human artifacts are not the only evidence of interest to the archaeologist. Today environmental archaeologists are interested in weather conditions prevailing in past times, in the crops grown, in insects and weeds, in the breed and size of domestic animals, poultry and cattle and in the diet of man. Such evidence comes in the form of minute particles of seed or from miniscule fragments of animal remains which can be examined closely under the microscope in the environmental laboratory. The climate of Jorvik was probably more similar to that of continental Europe today than to our present climate. The winters were colder and the summers warmer, but conditions in York were always humid and the buildings were surrounded by rotting rubbish. Under these unsavory conditions it is not surprising to learn that many of the citizens suffered from intestinal parasites the eggs of which are found in their excrement.

Nevertheless soon after the Danish Vikings invaded the Anglo Saxon city in 876 A.D. they were, by commercial enterprise, by first class seamanship, artistry, craftsmanship and vigour, soon to make it an important trading city in the centre of a Scandinavian commercial empire stretching from Russia in the east to Iceland and Greenland in the west and to the Arab lands in the south, a city to rival Hedeby in Germany,

Birka in Sweden and Dublin in Ireland. There was real evidence of this from Coppergate.

# THE JORVIK VIKING CENTRE

Such a wealth of finds has not been locked away in museum showcases. Jorvik Viking Centre, a museum of singular character, has been built on the actual archaeological site. Over part of the area excavated the buildings have been reconstructed as far as possible on their original alignment in order to give a realistic impression of life in the bustling Viking city, while the remaining part has been left as the archaeologists themselves left it, suggesting to the viewer the methods by which evidence of the past is obtained. In addition in the Skipper Gallery a selection of some of the smaller finds are displayed in show cabinets to illustrate the various aspects of everyday life and commerce in Viking time.

Visitors are conducted in time cars through the narrow alleys leading from Coppergate past people, past homes, workshops and warehouses towards the wharves of the River Foss. The bone carver sits surrounded by antlers and bones working to make combs, pins and the needles used to sew sailcloth. The cooper displays barrels used for transporting herrings or for salting meat, wooden buckets with rope handles, stools and cups and bowls turned from wood on a pole lathe. The jeweller sells plated brooches, bangles and rings from a stall outside his house and the leatherworker displays a good stock of hand sewn boots, slippers, belts and purses hung all round his stall.

A good impression is gained of life in the greatly overcrowded homes of ordinary folk, where everything was centred on the hearth. Here the bread was baked on a flat stone and here the barley meal and meat were stewed with carrots and beans in iron pots. Board games like Hnefatafl, in which the king, defended in his stronghold in the centre of the board by loyal companions, attempts to escape to the edge of the board outwitting the moves of attackers determined to capture him, were played, noisily and recklessly by the children, but with more cunning strategy and caution by their elders. At the wharf there is a cargo boat, recently docked from the Rhineland with wine and pots and skins and barrels of salted herrings stand untidily on the quayside ready for export.

In the homes women work with distaff and spindle twisting yarn from wool. Young girls weave patterned braids and the looms stand with bolts of herring-bone pattern tweed half woven. Every effort has been made to capture in addition to the visual impression the sounds and smells of the real city. Children recite riddles in old Norse, adults gossip and argue and an unpleasant odour drifts from a nearby latrine. Everywhere in yards choked with pigsties and pens are chickens, ducks and geese, snarling dogs and the occasional wary tabby cat. It is as realistic a reconstruction of a Viking city as one will ever see.

# STREET NAMES

It is in the naming of the city streets that Viking influence is most strongly shown today. The main street or great street is Micklegate, for 'mickle' means great. Coney Street was the Koenig Gate, where the royal hall was situated. Petergate led to St. Peter's Minster. Goodramgate took its name from Guthram. Stonegate followed the path of the Old Roman Via Praetoria and was the street through which stone to build a succession of Minsters was brought up from the quay on the River bank close by the abutment of the Roman bridge. No town in Britain has so many streets with Viking names as York. Jorvik reached a peak of prosperity in Viking times. How greatly was this city to suffer in the Norman invasion.

# Chapter Six

# THE NORMAN INVASION

# HAROLD ASSUMES THE CROWN

On Christmas Day 1065 the old and saintly Edward the Confessor lay dying. It had been his dearest wish to see his new abbey at Westminster consecrated. His last years had been occupied in supervising its re-building in the revived Romanesque style of architecture favoured by the Normans. As a boy he had lived at the Norman Court and he was much impressed by what he had seen there. Later in life some say he had given his relative William Duke of Normandy hope that one day he would be able to claim the English crown.

Now the abbey stood magnificently in the meadows by the side of the Thames, but the old king was not present with Witan to see the consecration. He lingered on in life until January 5th, 1066, when almost with his dying breath, he recommended the young and virile Harold Godwinson, son of Earl Godwin of Wessex,to the Witan as their choice for the throne of England. Harold was elected and on 6th,January he was crowned by Archbishop Stigant in the new abbey church, the first of the kings of England to be crowned there.

# THE PORTENTS AND RIVAL CLAIMANTS

Well might men wonder in the spring of 1066 at the sight of a bright star appearing curiously in the heavens! Was this a portent of evil things to befall the kingdom? In Normandy William felt himself cheated by Edward and betrayed by his rival Harold. A year or two previously Harold had been shipwrecked on the Channel coast of France and, while detained at the Norman Court, had sworn an oath of allegiance to Duke William, an oath made doubly binding by the proximity of the bones of holy saints enclosed in a box beneath the table in the hall of presence at Bayeux, where the oath had been sworn.

In Norway, Tostig, Harold's half brother, who had been exiled for misgovernment in the north, smarted at the side of Harold Hardrada, the Viking chief. Would this be the chance to re-establish the Viking kingdom of the north lost by Eric Bloodaxe? While King Harold's attention was occupied with preparations to repel a Norman invasion of the south coast, the Vikings prepared to attack the north.

# KING HAROLD'S PREPARATIONS

Harold assembled the Fryd, the Saxon army, along the south coast and the long wait throughout the spring and summer of 1066 commenced. Crops were sown throughout the land and soon the time of harvest came. Some Saxons, wearied by the waiting and mindful of the needs of winter, went home to gather the harvest, but still Harold waited.

In Normandy, Duke William first commended his cause to the Pope on the strength of Edward's promise to him and of Harold's broken oath. Help was forthcoming. In sending William a Holy Banner the Pope blessed his cause and William was able to appeal to barons, and knights from all over France, promising them the reward of new lands in England if they should help him to gain the kingdom.

Forests were cut down. Boats were built. Stores and provisions were assembled, arms and horses were collected and all were taken down to the sea and loaded on to the invasion fleet. Autumn had come and William's anxiety increased. Unless the wind changed to favour his adventure he might fail for he could not expect to bear the expense of maintaining such a force throughout the winter. Everything depended upon a favourable outcome before winter closed in.

# THE VIKINGS STRIKE FIRST

The same wind that kept William shorebound at St. Valery brought Tostig and Hardrada to the coast of Yorkshire in early September. Here they burned the coastal villages from Cleveland to Spurn Point and then sailed on the tide up the

Humber and Ouse to Riccal. They disembarked within striking distance of York, the second city in the land and the capital of the north. They brushed aside the Saxon Earls Edwin and Morcar at Fulford a mile from the city and then, rather than enter the walls, they withdrew to a more open defensive position at Stamford Bridge, ten miles away to the east, at a place where the Derwent was crossed by a narrow wooden bridge. Here they unfurled the Raven Banner and from here they sent messages inviting all Viking freemen of the north to join them, for the main Saxon onslaught would not be delayed.

# THE BATTLE OF STAMFORD BRIDGE

Harold the King was obliged to leave his watch on the south coast and to hurry north with his house carls collecting 'hatever extra forces he could on the march through the Midland shires. On September 25th, 1066 the Saxon army gathered under the Red Wyvern of Wessex to face the Vikings across the narrow muddy stream. There was a parley and the Vikings, who had not received the help they had expected from the freemen of the north, refused to yield.

Fighting was bitter. At first the Saxon spearmen could not gain a crossing for a stout Dane holding the bridge cut down many with his axe. Soon tactical advantage was achieved when he was speared from below by a Saxon in a boat. Harold's men streamed over the bridge to hurl themselves on the Viking axemen.

Tostig and Hardrada were both killed, earning their grant of land in England, sufficient only for their graves. Peace was negotiated. The dead were stripped of their weapons and items of value and their bodies buried. What was left of the Viking army was allowed to go home and Harold rejoiced for his victory in York. What was left of the once proud Viking fleet was last sighted by Northern freemen from Flamborough Head as it made through the rising swell to Norway. The sails billowed in the freshening wind. Cloaked stearsmen braced themselves at the starboard oars. Many warriors were wounded and there were scarcely enough able men huddled on the benches to ply the oars. But come what may, the Vikings would be back.

Axemen at Stamford Bridge

# THE NORMANS ARE HERE

As Harold hurried back to the south, news was brought to him that William had landed at Pevensey and that Normans were burning and pillaging the countryside round about. This was Harold's homeland Wessex. He made all possible speed to meet this new threat and by October 14th the Saxon forces, now much depleted, were in position on Senlac Hill overlooking the Normans.

# THE BATTLE OF HASTINGS

Critics argue strongly that it would have been to Harold's advantage to have waited until he could have collected superior forces, as he most assuredly would have been able to do. The Normans would have then been at a disadvantage, short of supplies, occupying an invasion beach head only and with the winter seas behind them. But Harold was flushed with victory. He could not see his beloved Wessex despoiled further and he chose to give battle at once.

All through the day Norman knights rode across the broken ground to throw themselves at the Saxon shield wall on the crest of the hill. Their valiant efforts were brought to naught by Saxon spears and axes. At one stage rumour passed through the Norman ranks that Duke William was dead, but the Duke rode out before them lifting his helmet that all might recognise his face. His half brother Odo, Bishop of Bayeux, laid about himself stoutly with mace and chain for his priestly office forbade the use of sword and Norman archers shot volley after volley of arrows high into the air to fall among the Saxon ranks.

As evening approached, the Normans caused the Saxons to break their ranks in pursuit of a feigned attack on the flank of their position and turning upon them cut them down. Almost at the same moment Harold was struck in the eye by an arrow and fell dying among his bodyguard, still urging them to stand firm and reform their broken ranks. The Saxons withdrew into the forest and William was in possession of the field. Fate had caught the luckless Harold, the oath-breaker.

# WILLIAM'S CORONATION

William did not feel sufficiently secure to march straight to London. He made a round-about approach along the coast to Dover and then by the northern edge of the Weald, securing Canterbury and Rochester before crossing the Thames at Wallingford to enter London from the north. The Saxon noteables met him at Berkhamstead and he was offered the crown. Even as he was crowned in Westminster Abbey on Christmas Day, 1066 by Aldred, Archbishop of York, his retainers outside, mistaking the loyal acclamations inside the abbey for sounds of revolt, set fire to houses round about which might harbour traitors. His position was tenuous and his supporters clearly touchy.

# REVOLTS IN THE NORTH

The pacification of England under Norman rule was not achieved without further desperate and bloody fighting. Nowhere was this fighting more bitter than in the north, where proud Anglo-Scandinavian freemen treasured their independence and nowhere did the Normans take their revenge more cruelly.

Three times William had to travel north to suppress revolts. Edwin and Morcar the Saxon Earls, who had sworn allegiance to him, betrayed him and William marched north, established a castle in York and appointed William Malet Sheriff and garrison commander. After a second revolt, William sacked the city and killed several hundred of its inhabitants. But in 1069, after an even more serious uprising supported by the Danes, in which the Norman garrison were slain beneath their defences, in bitter anger and rage William again rode north to kill every living thing in his path and to burn every town, village and hamlet. This was the 'Harrying of the North.' Thousands fled west of the Pennines or into Scotland. For those who escaped the fire and sword at home there was death by famine and disease. Hamlets and villages disappeared from the face of the earth from York to Durham traceable today in tussocks or hummocks of grass on moorland fringes or in the dales. Others survive as place-names on ancient maps. Badresby is now Battersby Barn Farm, Siwarthorpe and Tuislebroc are seen as field names and the manor of Falsgrave, which once had 108 freemen in 21 villages and 46 ploughteams, was reduced to a waste which supported only 7 freemen and 29 villeins or cottars operating 7 ploughs in 1086, seventeen years after the disaster. The Manor of Gilling in the North Riding, which had been worth 56 pounds a year in 1065, was worth only 24 in 1086 since most of it had reverted to waste land. In Wichistun just outside the City of York, where formerly there had been land for three ploughs to till, only one plough was at work and there was gorse and undergrowth half a league in length and half a league in breadth on former plough land. Yorkshire had become a wilderness fit only for Norman barons to hunt over.

# THE CITY OF YORK IN DOMESDAY TIMES

Twenty years after his conquest, because of the threat of invasion by King Cnut of Denmark, William wished to have all details of his Kingdom set down and an estimate made of the number of armed men he could call upon to fight and the amount of tax money due. With characteristic Norman efficiency all this was accomplished within one year. Instructions were given at the Great Court at Gloucester at Christmas 1085. Commissioners were sent throughout the whole country to enquire the value of land and property in the last year of King Edward's reign, its value in 1086, and its value on transfer of ownership, if this had changed in the previous twenty years. The Domesday record is less complete in the north, where the country was less densely populated and where the 'harrying of the north' had caused so much desolation. The extract for the City of York is interesting in so far as it shows the once proud and prosperous Viking trading capital just struggling back to relative prosperity in 1086. There are some interesting details concerning rights to possession of property and privileges and there is an account of the deliberate despoliation of one whole ward of the city and of much valuable farming and orchard land to build the twin castles and their associated defence works, which controlled the approach by river to the Vale of York.

In King Edward's time there had been seven wards or liberties in the city. By 1086 the Archbishop still controlled his own ward, but in the remaining five wards only 391 houses were regularly occupied, 400 were tenanted on occasion and 540 were empty and derelict. Frenchmen, the families of the garrison, occupied a further 145. The Canons of the Minster had their own freehold dwellings and so did the four judges to whom the King had given freeholds for as long as they lived.

The Bishop of Durham had a house which he had always occupied during his visits to York and which he claimed was rent free, but the burgesses said otherwise. He had paid rent in the time of King Edward. Perhaps the bishop had taken advantage of the troubled times to appropriate the freehold for himself!

The Norman Defences of York

The plight of a certain Uctred is mentioned. His house had been taken down and removed and re-assembled in the Castle Yard by William De Percy during the time of the revolts. Hugh the new Sheriff had ordered this demolition and Uctred presumably lost his house for ever, though he retained his title to the land on which it had stood.

Such great barons as the Count of Mortain, William de Percy and Ernis de Barun all held property in the city: churches and their estates, freehold dwellings and shops. These were sublet to lesser tenants and the names of their former owners: Sonulf, Morulf, Gamel, Sort, Turfin, Ligulf, Osbert, Ernui, Walcret, Dunstan, Grim and others are listed in the survey.

The farmland round the city, cultivated according to custom by the burgesses, had once extended to ploughland for 85 ploughs. Much of this was now waste and a good deal of land and two new water mills, once each worth 20 shillings a year, had been flooded when the Normans dammed the river Foss to raise the water level sufficiently high to fill the moat round the base of the castle tower. The King's Pool remained an impassable swamp to the north east of the city until the 19th century, when it was drained by Victorian engineers and built over. It was never reclaimed as agricultural land.

## SUMMING UP

The extent of misery and suffering caused by the 'Harrying of the North' will never be fully known. The Normans themselves did little to re-populate the county. This was accomplished eventually by natural increase of the original Anglo-Scandinavian stock and by the return of some of the refugees. The mark of the Normans could be seen in the wooden keeps erected by the Norman barons and knights to serve as strongholds for their families and retainers in their new lands. It is also seen in the system of land tenure they imposed which sought to deny freemen their ancient privileges and reduce them to servitude. They dwelt for many generations as an alien minority: the Percies, Laceys, de Buslis, de Warennes and others among a sullen though not dispirited peasantry.

Soon their wooden towers were rebuilt in grey stone and eventually former animosities were subdued by the more immediate threat of invasion by the Scots. The freemen, both Saxon and Viking, had given the Normans no easy victory in the north

## TRANSCRIPT OF THE DOMESDAY SURVEY EXTRACT FOR YORK

In the City of York in the time of King Edward, besides the ward of the Archbishop, there were six wards. One of these is cleared for the castles. In five wards there were 1,418 inhabited dwellings. Of one of these wards the Archbishop has yet a third part. In these no one else had freehold unless as a burgess, except Merlewsweyn, in a house which is within the castle, and except the Canons, wherever they dwelt, and except 4 Judges, to whom the King gave this gift by his writ and for so long as they live. But the Archbishop had full freehold of his ward.

Of all the above mentioned houses there are now inhabited in the hand of the King rendering rent, 400 less 9 great and small and 400 dwellings not regularly inhabited, which render, the better one penny and the others less, and 540 dwellings so empty that they render nothing at all and Frenchmen hold 145 dwellings.

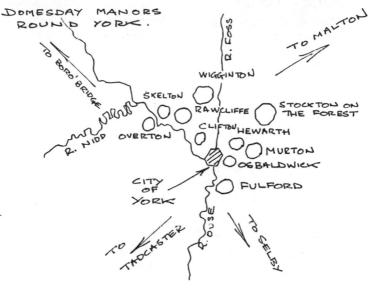

DOMESDAY MANORS ROUND YORK.

BY 1086 THE DISTRICT WAS ONLY JUST BEGINNING TO STRUGGLE BACK TO SOME SORT OF PROSPERITY AFTER THE HARRYING OF THE NORTH.

# THE LAND SURROUNDING THE CITY OF YORK

In the geld of the city there are 84 carucates of land and each of them rendered as much geld 'tax' as one house in the city. Of these the Archbishop has 6 carucates, which 3 ploughs can till. These belong to the farm of his hall. This land was not built up in King Edward's time, but cultivated in places by the burgesses, now it is the same. Of this land the King's pool destroyed 2 new mills worth 20 shillings a year, and of arable land and gardens and meadows nearly one carucate. In the time of King Edward it was worth 16 shillings, now it is worth 3 shillings.

# WIGGINTON A TYPICAL VILLAGE NEAR YORK

In Wichistun there are 3 carucates for geld which one plough may till. Saxford the Deacon held this, now St. Peter (the Archbishop) has it. It was and is waste. There is underwood there in the whole half a league in length and a half a league in breadth.

Clearly York had seen much depradation between 1066 and 1086 and was only just struggling back to affluence.

# PROPERTY IN THE HANDS OF NORMAN TENANTS-IN-CHIEF

St. Cuthbert (the Bishop of Durham) has one house which he always had, as many say quit of all rent, but the burgesses say that it was not quit in the time of King Edward.

Besides this house the Bishop of Durham has of the gift of the King, the church of All Saints' (Pavement) and what belongs to it, and the whole land of Uctred and the land of Ernuin which Hugh the Sheriff delivered to Bishop Walcher by the King's writ.

The Count of Mortain has here 14 dwellings and 2 stalls in the Shambles and the Church of St. Crux. Osbern, son of Boson has received these and whatsoever pertains to them. These dwellings had belonged to these men: Sonolf the priest 1, Morulf 1, Sterre 1, Esnarre 1, Gamel 1, Archil 5, Leuing the priest 2, Turfin 1, Ligulf 1.

William de Perci has 14 dwellings of these men: Bernulf, Selecolf, Odulf, Sonneve, Osbert, Gamelbar, Arlgrim, Welcret, Sort, Norman, Uchel, Egbert, Dunstan, Godelent, and the church of St. Mary (Castlegate) of Earl Hugh. William has 2 dwellings of two reeves of Earl Harold (Edwin and Morcar).

Moreover, concerning the dwelling of a certain Uctred, the burgesses say that William de Perci, removed it for himself into the castle ..... William however denies that he had the land of the same Uctred, but he says that, by direction of Hugh the Sheriff, he removed the house of Uctred into the castle in the same year as the destruction of the castle. (During the revolts against William).

Robert Malet has 9 dwellings of Tumme, Grim, Grimchetel, Ernui, Elsi, another Enui, Glunier, Halden and Ravenchel.

Ernis de Barun has 4 dwellings of Grim, Alwin, Gospatric and another Gospatric and the Church of St. Martin (Micklegate). Two of these dwellings rendered 14 shillings.

In the time of King Edward the city was worth to the King 53 pounds - now 100 pounds.

In the ward of the Archbishop, there were in the time of King Edward 200 inhabited dwellings less 11. Now there are 100 inhabited, great and small, besides the Court of the Archbishop and the houses of the Canons. In this ward, the Archbisop has as much privilege as the King has in his wards.

# Chapter Seven

# THE WORK OF THE MONKS IN YORKSHIRE

The eleventh century was marred by invasion, warfare and deliberate waste. By contrast, in the twelfth century we see the beginnings of reconstruction. In particular we notice the patient labour of the monks who were the real pioneers and leaders in this work.

## ST. BENEDICT

In Europe and the Near East from the very earliest times there had been Christian hermits living lonely ascetic lives dedicated to God. St. Benedict, an Italian in the early sixth century, gave order and earthly purpose to these lives for future centuries by channelling their effort into the community life of the monastery.

St. Benedict devised a rule by which monks could live together unselfishly in the service of God. They must pray and praise God eight times a day; they must study the holy scriptures and they must work with their hands. In this way they would achieve self discipline. A monk should have no use for wealth of his own, no time for a family of his own and no inclination for a will of his own. To be a monk he must take the vows of poverty, chastity and obedience. St. Benedict gave advice about the selection of young monks. If a young man presented himself at the monastery gate asking to become a monk he should not be let in too easily, but he should be kept waiting outside, perhaps in the guest house, for four or five days so that he should first learn patience. Then he could be admitted as a novice. After two months practice, when he had begun to understand the rule, he should be asked if he would observe it. If he agreed, after a further two years perseverance, the novice could be asked to make his final vows and would then be admitted as a monk. At this stage he would give up all his worldly goods to the Abbot and he would receive the habit of a monk, for each monastery was a family where all members helped each other.

# THE RULE OF ST. BENEDICT

The monk's life was not intended to be harsh or unpleasant and empty of joy. St. Benedict wrote at the beginning of his rule, 'We are now going to start a school for the service of God in which we hope nothing burdensome will be demanded. In living our life by the growth of faith the path of God's commandments is run with unspeakable loving sweetness.'

There were simple human rules to govern all conduct in the monastery. 'Wherever anything important has to be decided let the Abbot call together all the family of monks. After hearing their advice let him make up his own mind. Let the brothers give their opinions humbly and presume not stiffly to argue their own views.' This rule governed conduct in the chapter meeting. In the dormitory St. Benedict wrote, 'All monks shall sleep in separate beds. Let them all sleep in a common dorter. Let a candle be always burning till morning and let the monks sleep in their clothes. They shall always be ready to rise quickly when the signal is given and hasten to the Divine Office. The younger brothers are not to have their beds next to each other, but among those of the elders. And let them rouse the sleepy heads and help them to get up.'

Meals eaten by the monks were to be simple and plain. The brothers were to serve each other. 'No one may be excused from work in the kitchen. On Saturday, he who ends his weekly service must clean-up everything. He must wash the towels with which the brothers wash their hands and feet, and he who finishes his service and he who begins are to wash the feet of all the rest.'

The brothers were to practise silence at all times. They were to have simple clothing suitable to the climate and stockings and boots and they were not to grumble about the colour or rough material of their clothes. When getting new clothes they must always give back the old ones to be kept for the poor.

It was enough for a monk to have two habits to wear and two cowls, anything more was extravagant.

Only by observing the rule meticulously, argued St.

Benedict, could a monk come under God's guidance and attain the lofty heights of belief and virtue that would assure him of eternal life.

# THE MONK'S DAY

Timings for the main observances of the monk's day varied according to the hours of daylight throughout the year, but they always followed the same pattern. In winter time the brothers would be awakened at about 2 a.m. for the service of Vigils. Silently they would pass through the dim corridor from the dormitory and down the night stairs into the abbey church, where they would each take an appointed place in the choir stalls for this watch-night service. Novice and junior monks sat nearest the altar, older monks further back. Sometimes the Abbot or the Prior would walk softly round the stalls to rouse any sleepy heads during the long chants.

The time until sunrise was spent silently in the cloister or in the church, or perhaps in the warming house at the corner of the cloister. At dawn came the service of Matins or Lauds, a joyful service giving praise for the beginning of another day. At six a.m. came the service of Prime followed by a celebration of Mass at the high altar. Tierce came next and following this was the daily chapter meeting where all sat in order under the Abbot, to hear a chapter read from St. Benedict's rule. The souls of departed brethren would be remembered in prayer and, if it were a saint's day, prayers might be said to commend that saint. Any necessary business would be discussed and penances would be given to those who admitted to faults.

Chapter Meeting was usually followed by work in the cloisters until the service of Sext at mid-day. The next service, Nones, was said early in the afternoon and then followed the one meal of the day, although it must be said that young and growing monks, or lay brothers engaged in hard manual work in the fields, could have a simple meal of mixt earlier in the day. Vespers was said at dusk when the whole company of the abbey, monks and lay brothers, would gather in the cloisters before entering church. Compline would be said last of all at nightfall. The monks would retire to bed after this. The abbey bell which summoned the monks to their devotions was as regular as a clock striking the hours. It must have been a comfort to laymen in the sinful world outside the abbey precincts, to know that the monks were praying for the salvation of all men.

# THE MONASTERY BUILDINGS

The buildings of a monastery were perfectly designed for the life led by the monks. Foremost in importance and splendour was the abbey church with its nave, choir, presbytery and transepts. Each monk had his place and there was ample room for processions on important days. To the south were the cloisters, a square arcaded court where monks could walk, read or study in small wooden cubicles or carrels. Closest to the church on the eastern side of the cloister were the sacristy, where the altar furniture was kept, the vestry where chasubles, copes and other vestments hung and the library where psalters, missals and gospels used at the altar were stored. The chapter house stood in the centre of this walk and next to this was usually the parlour, a small room where a monk might talk, by appointment, to a visitor bringing news from the outside world.

Along the south face of the cloister were usually grouped the warming room and the refectory and kitchen. To complete the square on the west side were quarters for lay brethren or store rooms. The monks' dorter or dormitory usually ran along the eastern side of the cloister above the chapter house. Night stairs led down to the south transept of the church and day stairs to the cloister. Lay brothers slept in their own dorter on the west side of the cloister with their own stairs leading to the nave of the church. There was always an infirmary for sick or aged monks close by, and a meat kitchen for those prescribed meat meals by the infirmarian. In later years the Abbot frequently had a separate lodging and there was a gatehouse at the entrance to the abbey precinct. Just outside was a guest house for travellers.

# THE SPECIAL OFFICIALS OF A MONASTERY

The Abbot took responsibility for all the monastery, for the brethren and for lands and properties of the house. To assist him he had a prior and sometimes a sub prior who arranged the daily routine, seeing to the timings, speaking to those who might otherwise become slack in their ways and locking the doors after the monks had retired to sleep. In the morning he encouraged those who were inclined to over sleep, kept the monks from quarrelling and saw that the house was at peace.

The sacrist looked after the bread and wine for use at the altar and took care of the vestments, the altar frontals and the altar silver, candles and candlesticks. The precentor or cantor was a choir master, a very necessary responsibility for all the services were chanted and the standard must be high, for all was done for the greater glory of God. The librarian looked after the books and gospels, the refectorian saw that there were always clean rushes on the floor of the refectory and that napkins, spoons, cups and salt were placed on the tables. The almoner dispensed charities to the poor, who came daily to the abbey. The infirmarian cared for the sick and elderly monks or for elderly lay folks, who had given their property to the abbey thereby purchasing corrodies giving them the right to spend their remaining days in peace in the infirmary. The guestmaster or hospitaller saw to the running of the guest house, the master of novices instructed the young monks and there was a cellarer or kitchener to arrange all outside purchases and to see that there was always sufficient in store in the granary bins.

# THE DIFFERENT MONASTIC ORDERS IN YORKSHIRE

The first monasteries following the Rule of St. Benedict were Whitby, Selby and York St. Mary's. As time went on different orders were founded based upon slight variations of this rule. Poverty, chastity, obedience and hard work lead inevitably to riches, splendour and self indulgence. This became the fate

SOME MONASTERIES AND
PRIORIES IN YORKSHIRE.

WHITBY

GUISBROUGH

BRIDLINGTON

HULL

MEAUX

WATTON

WARTER

KIRKHAM

MALTON

NEWBURGH

BYLAND

RIEVAULX

ROSEDALE

MOUNT GRACE

EASBY

MARRICK

COVERHAM

JERVAULX

FOUNTAINS

MARTON

NUN MONKTON

YORK
ST. MARYS

NUN

HOLY TRINITY

APPLETON

SELBY

PONTEFRACT

NOSTELL

ROCHE

MONK
BRETTON

KIRKSTALL

ESHOLT

ARTHINGTON

BOLTON

SAWLEY

of many Benedictines. New orders, the Cluniacs and Cistercians, the latter founded by St. Robert of Molesme in 1098 and brought,after 1112,to perfection at Citeaux,by an Englishman St. Stephen Harding and a Burgundian St. Bernard, hoped to return to earlier stricter observances. Their habits were of white undyed cloth. The architecture of their churches was at first plain. Their altar frontals and vestments were of plain linen and their candlesticks of iron. There are many of their houses to be seen in Yorkshire, for they sought remote places. The most spectacular monastic ruins in Yorkshire today:Rievaulx, Fountains, Jervaux and Roche are all Cistercian houses, and there are others.

The two Carthusian Priories in the county are at Hull and at Mount Grace. The Carthusians were founded by St. Bruno at Chartreuse and,unlike other orders,they returned as far as possible to the early strictness of the hermit fathers. This made their priories different from the normal pattern. The church was unusually small because the monks lived and worshipped each in a separate cell. The cells were spaced round the cloister, which was therefore large. Each monk had his own walled garden next to his cell for meditation and work.

Finally there were the Austin Canons and the Premonstratensian Canons,who lived the community life of monks, but who had parochial responsibilities in nearby villages. Chaucer's worldly monk was an Austin Canon. Let us hope there were none so carefree and neglectful of their duties as he in Yorkshire.

Besides the monasteries there were also numerous nunneries, some, like Nun Monkton a Benedictine house, in country villages, others in towns, where no doubt the nuns often occupied themselves with charitable works.

# WHY THE REFORMED ORDERS CHOSE YORKSHIRE

Because of the wild untamed geography of much of Yorkshire in the middle ages and because of the desolation caused by the harrying of the north after the two risings of 1068 and 1069, there were many remote and desolate places where monks could find an ideal habitation. The story of Rievaulx and Fountains demonstrates this.

Fountains Abbey

# RIEVAULX

In 1131 Abbot William and his twelve followers, the first group of Cistercian monks in Yorkshire, passed through the City of York on their way to Ryedale, where Walter L'Espec, Constable of Helmsley, had granted them land. They were given hospitality by the worldly monks of St. Mary's. In Ryedale they were successful. They built a beautiful abbey and brought order and beauty to what must at first have been a hostile environment. They reached their most perfect age under St. Ailred, a young man in the service of the King of Scotland, who was so impressed by their zeal and saintliness that he decided to give up his diplomatic career and become a Cistercian monk. Ailred saw the monastery grow in size to a brotherhood of a hundred and forty monks and five hundred lay brethren. Under his direction the magnificent buildings were brought well on their way to completion and on saints' days, when all were assembled, the monastery buzzed with purposeful activity 'like a hive of bees.' Ailred, perhaps unlike St. Benedict, made it easy to join. The way to heaven had been found. It could be denied to no man. Old Walter L'Espec, his fighting days over, came to spend his last days with the monks. Sick or unhappy men, foreigners or fugitives came. If some were 'back sliders' there was always a penance and forgiveness. Ailred refused no one. 'All, weak or strong shall find a home here,' he said, 'like the fishes in a wide sea. There is peace and plenty of room.'

# FOUNTAINS

Abbot William and his twelve monks had a remarkable effect on the brethren at St. Mary's York. Some Benedictines, who had been greatly impressed by the zeal of the Cistercians, approached their Prior Richard to speak to Abbot Godfrey with a view to returning to a more strict rule in their house. They pointed out to the Abbot that it was the custom of St. Mary's to wander about chatting, they ate forbidden delicacies, they drank delightful wines, which they were really forbidden to touch, they lost their tempers and quarrelled, they pleased themselves about their religious observances, they made merry and grew fat.

But Godfrey was an old man who enjoyed his comfort and he refused to change. He even threatened to punish the dissatisfied monks for raising the matter. The brethren next approached Archbishop Thurstan, who visited the monastery with a crowd of priests from the Minster. There was a disgraceful scuffle as they tried to get into the chapter house, which was barred against them, and eventually the Archbishop had to withdraw, taking Prior Richard and his twelve followers with him to Ripon. On Christmas Day, 1132 Thurstan found the monks land in inhospitable Skeldale and they took possession in mid-winter, sheltering under the trees and facing starvation. Soon they were joined by Hugh, Dean of York a man of property. Their fortunes changed they appealed to St. Bernard for admission to the Cistercian order and in 1134 they were accepted as a daughter foundation. St. Bernard sent Geoffrey, a master mason, to help design and build their church, the nave of which stands in ruins today.

# THE ECONOMIC IMPORTANCE OF THE WORK OF THE MONKS IN YORKSHIRE

We can only understand the importance of the work of the monks if we realise the extent to which the country was despoiled by the 'harrying of the north'. Between York and Durham every habitation had been made desolate. Wild animals ran in the ruins of the villages. The Domesday Survey some seventeen years after showed the City of York and the surrounding district only slowly recovering prosperity. Most of the country was fit only for outlaws or for hunting. In the midst of this stood the grim fortresses of the new Norman landowners. But this was the very situation which attracted the new orders of monks.

# LAY LANDLORDS ENCOURAGE THE MONKS

There was no lack of assistance from landowners. It may have been considered by many good insurance to have the grateful brethren praying for their immortal souls. More-over the work done by the monks could bring peace and profit to areas of waste. Grants of land were freely made in the most desolate places. The Priory at Kirkham was founded in a deep overgrown gorge by Walter L'Espec of Helmsley some time between 1122 and 1130 for the Austin Canons.

He was buried there. Later it became the principal resting place of the Lords of Helmsley from William de Roos, who was buried in the presbytery in 1258, to his great grandson who was buried close by the high altar in 1345. The Lords Fitzhugh of Richmond, who granted lands in Wensleydale to the monks of Jervaulx, were buried from 1161 to 1386 at Jervaulx Abbey and there are many similar burials elsewhere. Kirkstall Abbey was founded by Henry de Lacy, grandson of Ilbert who had come with the Conqueror, in thanksgiving for deliverance from a serious illness and Roche was founded by Richard, Lord of Tickhill and Richard, son of Turgis, both of whom wished to be remembered in the prayers of the monks.

# THE MONKS AS PIONEERS

Norman landowners were trained to fight. They were not generally in the forefront of peaceful pursuits. The only educated people were in a monastery. The monasteries attracted the best brains of the community and provided a leaven to the mass of the people. The Cistercians in particular, because of their willingness to accept all as lay brothers, enabled many a renegade or fugitive to lead a useful life. The monks were leaders in domestic architecture, water supply and hygiene. But their greatest contribution was in the improvement of agriculture, where their knowledge of land clearing, drainage and animal husbandry served as an example to be copied by lay men.

# THE MONKS AT JERVAULX AND THEIR WORK IN WENSLEYDALE

The early history of the monks of Jervaulx illustrates this. In pre-conquest times at the lower end of the dale below Askrigg a fairly stable farming pattern, based upon cultivation of oats, barley and peas on lynchets or terraces, had been established. There was meadow land for hay and common pasture on the hills. Higher in the dale, beyond Askrigg, there was rough moorland and forest suitable for summer pasture or 'saetrs' of the Viking pattern, the 'setts' in modern place names. The Norman conquest had brought all this to an end. Perhaps the villages were destroyed or the inhabitants had fled. The ownership of vast areas was handed to Norman landowners and became a hunting forest. The Domesday Survey notes that in 1086 Askrigg had only five ploughs operating on arable land where formerly ten had worked.

In 1146 however came the beginning of change. Some monks of the order of Savigny, later to become Cistercians, were granted land at the dale-end at Fors near Bainbridge by

Earl Alan of Richmond. Soon they had five ploughs at work, some forty cows, sixteen mares with foals, five sows with litters, three hundred sheep, thirty hides in their tannery and wax and oil sufficient in store for two years. They had ale, butter, cheese and grain for bread sufficient until the next harvest - a not inconsiderable effort. But because of bad weather they lost their grain and suffered hardship.

In 1156 they left their rather exposed site for a better one just below East Witton, the present site of Jervaulx Abbey. Their subsequent skilful management settled the development of farming in Wensleydale for many years on the basis of cattle, sheep, pigs and horses. They set to work enclosing new pastures, clearing new land near the streams for meadows and draining marshy places. By 1301 they had ten farms or granges north of the River Ure and the sole pasture rights in the hills from Askrigg to the dale head. This was Abbot's Side. The south side was controlled by Middleham Castle.

The monks at Jervaulx excelled in horse breeding. Their stud was described as,'the tryed breed of the north, whereof the like was not to be found elsewhere.' At Rigg under Cottar-End they kept two stallions and 'ambling mares.' These were horses with a trotting gait, valuable at the time as palfreys, and the abbot and his monks could, no doubt, often be seen riding along the tracks on Abbot's Side, their harness jingling clearly in the cool wind.

Of sheep the monks of Jervaulx kept two breeds. One was small, hardy and black faced, giving coarse wool and able to live on the higher more exposed pastures. The other was larger, white faced and less hardy, but with softer, more valuable fleece. They had also mastered the skill of cheese-making from ewes' milk.

Their activities were not entirely directed to agriculture however. In 1250 John de Walton recognised their title to the iron ore workings of Colsterdale, lower in the dale and in 1334 Geoffrey de Scrope granted them the right to burn charcoal there for an annual rent of 8 marks.

Their lead in all these matters was closely followed by the estates of Middleham Castle.

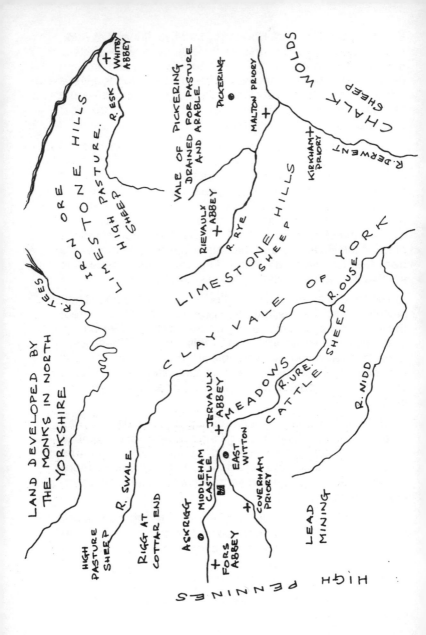

LAND DEVELOPED BY THE MONKS IN NORTH YORKSHIRE

IRON ORE HILLS

LIMESTONE HIGH PASTURE SHEEP

R. ESK

+ WHITBY ABBEY

R. TEES

HIGH PASTURE SHEEP

R. SWALE

RIGG AT COTTAR END

ASKRIGG ⊙

MIDDLEHAM CASTLE 🏰

EAST WITTON

JERVAULX + ABBEY

+ COVERHAM PRIORY

+ FORS ABBEY

HIGH PENNINES

LEAD MINING

MEADOWS

CLAY VALE OF YORK

CATTLE SHEEP

R. URE

R. NIDD

R. OUSE

R. RYE

RIEVAULX + ABBEY

LIMESTONE HILLS SHEEP

VALE OF PICKERING DRAINED FOR PASTURE AND ARABLE

PICKERING ⊙

MALTON PRIORY +

KIRKHAM + PRIORY

R. DERWENT

CHALK WOLDS

CHALK SHEEP

# THE DEVELOPMENT OF NORTH EAST YORKSHIRE

Similarly, the north east of the county was developed by the monks of Whitby, Guisborough, Rievaulx and Malton, houses which had gained wide estates within fifty years of the Domesday survey.

The land was geographically varied. Vast areas were high moorland. Many parts, including the deep clay-lined valleys cutting into the moorland, were virgin forest. Some areas had once been tilled, but had now gone to waste and much of the Vale of Pickering was marshy. Sometimes depopulated villages like Griff, Stilton, Deepdale and Loftmarshes became new monastic granges. In other places like Great Broughton and Winteringham, monastic granges were established alongside villages recovering from the devastation.

## ARABLE LAND

The best arable land was on a belt of fertile soils along the northern and southern edges of the Vale of Pickering. There, Malton Priory had several granges, Winteringham, Swinton, Sutton, Rillington, Thorpe and Amotherby, where wheat, barley, oats, rye and peas were grown and where monastic success served to help along lay men with similar crops.

In the centre of the vale in the marshy area, Loftmarsh and Keldmarsh granges, belonging to the monks of Rievaulx, were being drained and brought into cultivation so successfully that by 1274 the grange at Keldmarsh had three hundred acres of arable and a further three hundred acres of pasture and the Abbots of Rievaulx were still acquiring lands within the marsh to drain.

## SHEEP FARMING

Sheep farming by the monks was more important in the north east than any other activity. Flocks were large. Towards the end of the thirteenth century there may have been as many as sixty thousand sheep in the area belonging to the monks.

Rievaulx and Bridlington held as many as ten thousand each. The abbots did business on a large scale with Pegolotti and other Italian merchants and with merchants from Germany and the Low Countries. In addition they handled business on behalf of lay estates. This great pasture of sheep laid the foundation of modern pastoral farming in the area.

# THE MONKS' KNOWLEDGE OF CORRECT LAND USE

Wherever they had influence the monks gave a lead. They started settlements on moorland and marshland, showing what was possible. Other times they improved and developed what was already there, as in the arable areas surrounding the Vale of Pickering. Their agriculture was carefully adapted to the land itself and because of this it was successful.

# INDUSTRY IN THE NORTH EAST

The monks understood the smelting of iron and lead. They burned charcoal, they made tiles, and they could mine coal. The abbey churches of Rievaulx, Jervaulx, Byland and Fountains required a great deal of lead for roofs and for setting windows. Their tiled floors, fragments of which can still be seen, were a wonder at the time. The Abbot of Rievaulx gained a good income from the iron workings in the Cleveland Dales, where Adam Fitzpeter had granted him mineral rights. Guisborough Priory exploited similar rights in Glaisdale. Here perhaps was the start from which modern metallurgical industries have grown. The raw materials of industry were there. The early skills in working them were developed under monastic guidance and it may be true to say that the traditional skills in metalworking today were already being encouraged in the thirteenth century by the monks.

# CONCLUSION

In their hey-day the achievements of the monks in Yorkshire were great. They taught the fundamentals of religion. They gave the peasant a lead to follow in dark days and they led many to a fuller life than they would otherwise have enjoyed.

Their monasteries and priories were a refuge for the traveller, the poor, the sick and the old. They were foremost in the economic development of a devastated land and their monasteries were the technical schools of the age. They taught the ignorant countrymen rural crafts and the skills of husbandry and industry. Nowhere in England was this more important at the time than in Yorkshire.

Mount Grace Priory

# DAILY ROUTINE OF A CARTHUSIAN BROTHER AT MOUNT GRACE PRIORY

| | |
|---|---|
| 5.45 a.m. | Roused by the 'excitator,' performs toilet, recites first offices for the day in his cell. |
| 6.30 a.m. | Recites second 'Angelus' arranges his cell. |
| 6.45 a.m. | To church for High Mass. |
| 7.45 a.m. | Private Mass in his cell oratory. |
| 8.45-10 a.m. | 30 minutes meditation in his cell and afterwards 30 minutes manual labour. |
| 10.00 a.m. | Office said in his cell, followed by dinner and manual labour. |
| 12.00 noon | Recites 'third Angelus,' followed by manual labour. |
| 2.30 p.m. | Recites office in cell. |
| 2.45 p.m. | To church for 'Vespers'. |
| 4.00 p.m. | Returns to his cell. |
| 4.30 p.m. | Supper. |
| 6.00 p.m. | 'Fourth Angelus,' said in his cell. |
| 6.30-7 p.m. | Retires to rest. |
| 10.30-11 p.m. | Awakened by 'excitator' and recites his office in his cell. |
| 11.15-11.45p.m. | To church for 'night office.' |
| 2.15 a.m. | 'First Angelus' in church, returns to cell and recites short office. |
| 2.30 a.m. | Retires to rest, until about 5.45 a.m. |

The Carthusians, in contrast with other orders, attempted to combine the solitary life of a Christian hermit with the communal life of a monk. The greater part of the monk's day was spent alone in his cell. Even meals were taken in solitude. An angled serving hatch was built into the wall of each cell so that the monk did not see the face of the servant who brought his meals.

In contrast with other monasteries the Priory Church was small and the cloister, which had to accommodate the cells and private gardens, was very large.

## De Utensilibus Celle
### (About the furnishing of a Carthusian Monk's Cell)

The cell was a substantial building about the size of a modern house. The inmate of each cell received:- for his bed - a pallet, a felt if it can be had, a pillow, a quilt or covering of coarse sheep skin covered with coarse cloth. For his clothing - two hair shirts, two tunics, two pilches, one worse, the other better, likewise two cowls, three pairs of boots, four pairs of socks, a cap, night shoes and day shoes, fat also for greasing them, two lumbars, a girdle-all of canvas and coarse.

And whatsoever directly belongs to the bed or clothing of whatsoever colour or thickness it be, be he cloisterer or prelate, he shall not mind. Nevertheless it is lawful for priors and others going beyond the bounds, to have clothes a little better and for necessity lighter than those who stay at home, in which, as in all other things, all curiosity and niceness shall be avoided. For among all monks, and especially among us, it is ordered that meaness and coarseness of clothes and everything else we use be worthless and poor and our mood be one of self abasement.

The inmate of a cell also has: two needles, threads, scissors, a comb, a razor for the head, a hone or stone and a strop for sharpening.

For writing: a desk, pens, chalk, two pumices, two inkhorns, a penknife, two razors or scrapers for scraping parchment, a pointer, an awl, a weight, a rule, a ruler for ruling, tables, a writing style. But if a brother be of another craft, which very rarely happens among us, for almost all whom we receive, if it can be done, we teach to write, he has suitable tools for his craft.

And there are given him: two pots, two plates, a third for breads and a lid for it, and there is a fourth, somewhat bigger for washing up, two spoons, a knife for bread, a flagon, a cup, an ewer, a salt, a pan, a towel, tinder for his fire, fuel, strike-a-light, wood, a chopper, but for work an axe.

It will be seen that, though the Carthusian monk lived a solitary life, his life was intended to be industrious.

# Chapter Eight

# TRADE IN MEDIEVAL YORKSHIRE

## THE GROWTH OF NEW TOWNS IN THE 12th and 13th CENTURIES

The economic growth which took place in the l2th and l3th centuries brought many towns and villages into being. In Yorkshire the spread of people to the Pennine Dales and the north east led to new clearings and new villages and encouraged the development of new markets. Elsewhere in the county the steady improvement of existing arable areas increased the prosperity of existing markets. In some places such as Pateley Bridge, since the new colonists were employed in mining, the new market town dealt with a much wider range of goods than food and cattle.

We must not think of the peasant as being absolutely tied to the manor at this time. There were opportunities for enterprising souls to travel to nearby towns to seek employment.provided the correct fee was paid to the Lord of the Manor. The rolls of the Freemen of York seem to confirm this,for the earliest lists contain the names of many freemen who bore the name of their village or manor of origin as a surname. New towns brought increased revenue to landlords: burgage rents, market tolls, the profits of merchants' courts and the purchase price of liberties. It was therefore in the interest of everyone that urban development should be encouraged.

## THE FACTORS WHICH GOVERN THE SITING OF MARKETS

Peasants could market small surpluses of produce privately within the village. When they had larger surpluses to sell, however, they preferred to sell in town market places. In town there were standard weights and measures. There were more buyers and goods from other farms and manors could be compared for quality by buyer and seller alike before a fair price was struck. Moreover a wider range of manufactured goods were on show for sale in town. Most villages had blacksmiths, cobblers, bakers, brewers and carpenters. The goods and products of glovers, dyers, tailors, cordwainers, spicers and tinsmiths were only available in town. A visit to the town market, besides being a social event, was essential if something were needed.

Henry de Bracton, the l3th century lawyer, employed a great deal with legal cases concerning markets, observed that it was reasonable for a peasant to spend about one third of the day travelling to market with his cart or pack horse, one third of the day in marketing his produce and making his own purchases and the remaining one third of the day for his return journey to his village. It would follow then that markets could serve something in the nature of a six mile radius and that therefore towns or villages with markets would be spaced a little over this distance apart. It helped if markets were held on different days of the week in adjacent towns so that merchants of salt, spices or wool, who of necessity travelled greater distances, could visit each market town in turn, making good use of their time.

There were many fair-sized market towns in Yorkshire like Richmond, Beverley, Knaresborough, and Wakefield. There were an even greater number of smaller centres like Sheriff Hutton and Easingwold, whose ample stretches of open green today once provided the space for markets and fairs. If some of them have lost that importance it is because, in the hey-day of arable farming in the 13th century, rather too many markets were founded to be sustained in the more restricted times of the following centuries and so they closed. Because of the improvement of transport in modern times we do not need so many small markets and they have never revived.

# MARKETS IN THE CITY OF YORK

Markets have been held from time immemorial in York. York was a king's market, hence the right to hold it was rented from the King. There was no charter. The usual market places were 'the Pavement,' the only cobbled street in the city, and St. Sampson's Square by St. Sampson's Church. A small sea-fish market was held at Foss Bridge close by the confluence of the rivers Foss and Ouse. The fresh water fish market was held at King's Staith, close by the old Ouse Bridge. The market for malt was held in Coney Street and the butter market was in Micklegate.

Markets were for 'foreign' traders or those living out-side the city. Only outsiders were allowed to sell in the markets. City tradesmen sold in their shops and were not allowed to have market stalls. There was price-control in the markets, since the criterion in the middle ages was fair trade rather than cut-throat competition. Market traders were consequently not allowed to undercut the prices charged by city tradesmen. There was also quality control and the gild searchers were empowered to sample and test merchandise. Dishonest traders were fined and imprisoned for infringements.

On 14th April, 1553, Bernard Horner a butcher was brought before the Lord Mayor and Council for selling 'corrupt and stinking meat' and was committed to prison for it. Simon Foxgale and John Smith, both gild searchers, who should have been more diligent in their office to prevent this disgraceful state of affairs, were also sent to prison for neglect of duty. A short while afterwards four fishmongers were sent to prison for five weeks for soaking 'stock fish,' which was dried fish, in water mixed with lime to whiten it and make it appear fresh.

Forestalling was another offence regarded as a serious matter. All produce and merchandise brought to market had to pay normal market tolls. If however a would-be purchaser could meet the producer outside the city walls as he made his way to market, a private bargain might be struck for a load of malt, hay or other produce and the market tolls could be avoided. Any persons seen to be acting in a suspicious manner, deep in conversation by the roadside or striking a bargain outside the market would render themselves liable to prosecution for this offence.

The simple rules governing markets in York were similar to those which regulated markets all over the country. They were well understood by traders and purchasers and they were very sensible in their way.

# FAIRS AS MARKETS

The church, local landowners and cities sponsored many fairs in the Middle Ages. They were usually held on the eve of saints' days and on the saints' days themselves. The crowds who came to the fairs would normally visit the shrines in churches and abbeys and give money for their upkeep. Between 1227 and 1514 no fewer than a hundred and fifty seven fair charters were granted in Yorkshire. This does not give us a complete tally of the number of fairs however, because many towns had fair charters before 1227 and many held fairs without charters by ancient custom - 'time immemorial.' There may have been as many as three hundred fairs held in Yorkshire, some lasting only one day, others running on up to eight days and that at Hull continuing for the record time of thirty days.

The Lordship or ownership of a fair was a valuable privilege, for the Lord collected tolls on all goods brought into the fair and on all goods taken out. In addition he collected 'stallage' or rent of usually 2 pence for each seven-foot stall. The owner of the fair had certain responsibilities. He had to guarantee safety and justice for merchants and buyers alike. The fair court or 'Court of Pied Poudre' or dusty feet was usually set up for the duration of the fair, because disputes must be settled at once. Merchants would be anxious to move off promptly at the end of the fair. They would not wish to be detained in bringing disputes to court. In York the Archbishop held such a court at his Lammas fair. The city fairs however needed no such extra courts since disputes could be settled immediately in the city courts.

There was always a 'Clerk of the Market' appointed by the King to collect royal tolls, to see that the standard weights and measures were used and to attend to the assize 'testing' of bread and beer. On occasion, a fair owner might buy a charter enabling him to appoint his own Clerk. The City of York obtained such a charter from Edward II on 24th June, 1316, which confirmed their right to this privilege and proved that it was a privilege held by the city from earlier times. The original grant has been lost.

# FAIRS IN THE CITY OF YORK

A number of fairs were held in York, some by the city and one by the Archbishop. The 1449 charter of the city confirms the right of the city to hold a fair to commence each year on Whit Monday and to last five days more. Then in 1501, because the citizens were concerned at the increasing amount of business going to Hull, to the detriment of York, the city petitioned the King for two more fairs. One was to be held from the Monday after Ascension Day for eight days and the other from St. Luke's Day for eight days. These were both authorised, but the period was shortened in each case to six days. They were very quickly advertised in Malton, Scarborough, Richmond, Beverley, Hull, Doncaster, Rotherham, Halifax, Wakefield, Leeds, Northallerton and Helmsley so that merchants would be attracted.

The Archbishop's Lammas fair, which was well established by ancient custom before 1140,opened promptly at 3 p.m. on 3lst July and closed at the same time on the 2nd of August. The Archbishop took over responsibility for the whole administration of the city throughout this time and collected all tolls at the gates. This jurisdiction was surrendered to the Archbishop each year with some ceremony. The Archbishop's Steward, with two other gentlemen specially appointed and with 13 of the Archbishop's tenants from the Liberty of Wistow, one of the Archbishop's estates near Selby, who were to act as jury in all disputes, attended the courthouse on the old Ouse Bridge. Here, as soon as the bell of St. Michael's Church, Spurriergate, at the other end of the bridge, struck three, the Archbishop's Steward presented the Archbishop's patent for the fair to the two Sheriffs of the city. The Sheriffs then delivered their rods of office to the Archbishop's two gentlemen, who were to temporarily assume their office; conducted them round the adjoining prison and did all such other small duties necessary for giving over the administration of the city to their care. A similar ceremony marked the closure of the fair,when the Archbishop's Steward surrendered his responsibility to the city Sheriffs.

# CONDUCT OF THE FAIR

The fair was not a free for all. There were regulations governing the setting-up of the stalls and the sale of livestock and commodities. The first two days of the fair were given over to the sale of cattle and sheep. The remaining four days were for general merchandising. During the Ascension-Day fair, cattle were sold in Fishergate, riding horses were sold outside Walmgate Bar and sheep were sold on Hewarth Moor, one of the city strays. Fine southern cutting-cloth was sold in the Common Hall, the Guildhall today. Leeds, Halifax, Wakefield and Bradford cloth was sold in the street between the Common Hall and Stonegate, the area occupied by St. Helen's Square today. Kendal, Ripon and Knaresborough cloth was sold in Coney Street. Linen was sold in Patrick Pool and Jubergate. Wool, bread, meat and salt were sold in the Thursday market place. Fletchers, mattress makers, bedsellers, upholsterers, tapestry makers and anyone who worked with feathers traded in Goodramgate. Tanners and barkers went to Peasholme Green and cordwainers, or shoemakers, went to St. Saviourgate. Pewterers, founders, potters and metalworkers met in Colliergate, but ironmongers did business in Fossgate. Hat makers, tailors, saddlers, glovers, turners, coopers, cartwrights, hemp-sellers and ropers all traded in Walmgate, which was a long street, and cooks, poultrymen and victuallers were in Davygate and Swinegate. During a fair the whole city seemed to be taken over by merchants and visitors. The venues for trading for the second fair, the St. Luke's Fair, were different, no doubt to give the different trades the opportunity to occupy the best possible trading sites in turn. They were all set-down and allocated in the same detail.

# PORTS

Because land transport was so slow any settlements on rivers or estuaries stood a good chance of being developed as ports, especially in the 12th and 13th centuries, when coastal and overseas trading was developing. York was an important staple-port for the export of wool and had a Gild of Merchants. On the Humber estuary Grimsby was important as early as the Norman Conquest. But by the end of the 13th century the

Archbishop of York and several local magnates were developing other outlets. The most important of these was Wyke on Hull founded originally by the Abbot of Meaux and renamed Kingston-upon-Hull by Edward I in 1293.

# SETBACKS TO TRADE IN THE 14TH CENTURY

The Black Death and outbreaks of the plague that followed affected economic development all over Europe for a short while. In Yorkshire at Bolton near Bradford for example, not a soul remained to greet the tax collectors in 1379. Soon marginal land went out of cultivation as the remaining peasants moved to more attractive holdings now vacant. The landlords offered more favourable conditions of tenure to encourage this and the abandoned areas of poor soil were turned over to grass to meet the needs of the expanding market in wool.

Many of the new towns suffered. They had been built as a speculation. They had been profitable for a while but now their prosperity was at an end and they began to stagnate. In one isolated case nature also took a hand. Ravensrod had been built as a port off Spurn Point in the Humber estuary, where waves had thrown up sandbanks which provided a site. However no sooner was the port built than the capricious waves washed it away again.

# THE EFFECT OF PASTORAL FARMING ON SETTLEMENT

Sheep were folded on good arable land first in the 14th century. The shift from arable to pastoral farming that was to increase in intensity throughout the next two centuries was to have far reaching consequences. Because of the great demand for wool and because of the profit that could be made by selling it, landlords, especially after the dissolution of the monasteries, turned over the arable land of whole villages to sheepfolds and evicted the husbandmen. Sometimes the grassed-over sites of their homes remain as at Wharram Percy alongside the ruins of their church. There, recent excavation has uncovered the chalk rubble foundations of half-timbered peasants' longhouses, evacuated at this time, and in which family and cattle once shared the same roof. Wharram Percy is typical of many such deserted villages for the husbandmen have never returned and the ruined walls of the church stand among tussocks in the quiet fields.

# WILLIAM DE LA POLE - A YORKSHIRE MERCHANT

William de la Pole, a merchant of Hull, was one of the best business men of his time. Certainly the monks of Meaux Abbey, with whom he traded in wool, regarded him as 'second to no English merchant.' As a business man he was self seeking and unscrupulous, bent only upon his own gain. As a banker to the king he rivalled the Italians, lending Edward III as much as 111,000 pounds during 1338 and 1339 and securing repayment out of deliveries of royal wool. He was an important member of a small group of rich merchants who were profiting by the Scottish wars, provisioning armies and garrisons and becoming increasingly familiar with the king and his ministers. Finally he helped to change the free trade in wool into one controlled by the influential company of the English Merchants of the Staple to the great profit of that company and of the Crown, which raised taxes on the trade.

# THE SKILL OF A WOOL MERCHANT

There was a great deal of skill to be learned in the medieval wool trade. The wool merchant must be able to judge the quality of fleeces from different parts of the country and to make his own purchases of the different grades to suit foreign markets. There was considerable choice in the method of transport from producer to foreign buyer and some difference in the rates charged for this transport. Agents abroad to represent the wool merchants had to be selected carefully and paid according to their worth. Consignments of wool also, on occasion, had to be stored to advantage in England at the ports, or else abroad, until the wool could be sold at the best price. In normal times a reasonable profit could be made by the merchants. In time of war, or when high taxes were imposed upon the trade, these profits could dwindle or be lost altogether. William de la Pole's business career illustrates the importance of personal skill, knowledge of the markets and a certain commercial ruthlessness at a time when such expertise was rare among Englishmen.

# THE DISTRICTS FROM WHICH DE LA POLE PURCHASED WOOL

De la Pole bought wool at Blyth in Nottinghamshire,where some of the best monastic wool in the country was obtainable. This wool was worth 19 marks a sack in Flanders. His purchases of Lincolnshire wool were made from the district round Lincoln and from the Wolds. His Yorkshire wool was bought mainly from Swaledale, Wensleydale and Ryedale. He stored fleeces in Richmond, Northallerton and Myton-on-Swale close to the wool producing abbeys of Jervaulx, Rievaulx, Fountains and Byland. At the peak of the market good Fountains wool fetched twenty one marks a sack in the Flemish market whereas that of Rievaulx and Byland fetched seventeen and a half marks and that of Jervaulx seventeen. On average, year by year and taking into account fluctuations in the market, de la Pole must have sold at about seventeen and a half marks a sack. The skill came in making purchases of the different grades judiciously to meet precise market trends.

# TRANSPORT OF THE WOOL

De la Pole purchased his fleeces within reasonable distance of Hull. He paid six pence per sack for shipment by river from York to Hull, although some merchants had been known to manage this for as little as four pence a sack on occasion. Shipment from Bawtry to Hull by river cost him one shilling per sack, although royal wool from as far afield as Derbyshire was shipped to Hull for ten pence. Specially favourable terms were obviously quoted for the movement of the King's wool. Other merchants were known to have paid fifteen pence a sack from Bawtry to Hull.

De la Pole did not own warehouses in Hull but his accounts show that he did store wool there for a half penny per week per sack. This was a reasonable price.

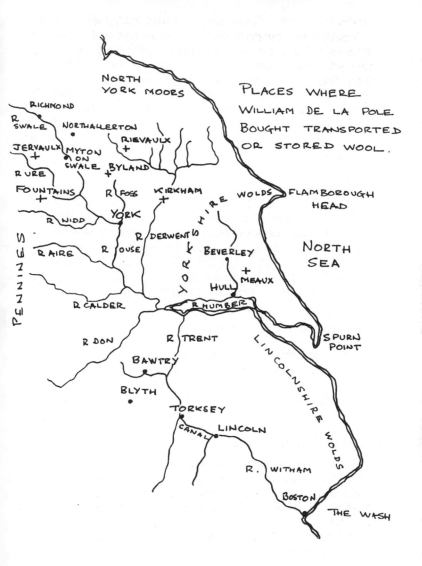

PLACES WHERE WILLIAM DE LA POLE BOUGHT TRANSPORTED OR STORED WOOL.

Like all merchants De la Pole did not export all his wool in one ship. The danger of ship-wreck or from pirates was too great. His cargo was always distributed over several ships, each sack being marked with his woolmark. In 1337 he spread his consignment from Hull over twelve different ships. He used two ships for a smaller cargo from Boston. Freight rates from Hull to Flanders varied between five and six shillings per sack depending upon whether the wool ships were to be accompanied, in troublesome times, by an escort of ships equipped for war, for these had to be paid for in addition to freight charges.

The expense of unloading wool in Dortrecht in 1337 was abnormally high because new equipment had to be brought into the town to weigh the unusually large shipment. Because of the shortage of warehouse space the cost of storage was also as high as three halfpence per sack per week. This is where the appointment of skilful and honest agents was an advantage and De la Pole's agents spent fifty five pounds on renting five warehouses. Other merchants may not have done so well.

# PAYMENT OF AGENTS

De la Pole employed more agents overseas than some other merchants and sometimes he paid them more generously for their trust. Each of his five agents received forty five shillings a month in 1338, whereas agents employed by other merchants were sometimes paid as little as twenty two shillings. But De la Pole preferred to employ men of exceptional experience, especially when times were difficult.

In 1339 three of his agents were in Bruges and their salaries at one shilling a day were closer to the average paid by other merchants. On their master's behalf they hired eight warehouses for sixty five weeks at ten pounds a year for each. De la Pole paid out a hundred pounds in warehouse charges but he shipped two-thousand, four hundred and nine sacks of wool and storage costs were as low as a sixth of a penny per week for a sack.

The average price of wool on the Flemish market in 1339 was only six pounds fifteen shillings a sack, but De la Pole's agents moved sixty one sacks of his Lincolnshire wool to Antwerp in December, at a cost of six pounds sixteen shillings and six pence for transport. The expense was justified because the wool sold at one pound thirteen shillings and four pence a sack more than the average on the Flemish market and a handsome profit was made with wool that would otherwise have stuck on the market.

# THE PROFITABILITY OF THE TRADE

The profit to be made in the wool trade was governed by the law of supply and demand, which caused normal market fluctuations. However, there were additional difficulties with which merchants had to deal, such as the arrival of particularly large shipments of 'royal wool.' The King invariably wanted to sell at once whereas prudent merchants would have put the wool on the market sufficient at a time to maintain the price. When the king's wool flooded the market the market price always fell causing merchants concern.

Very few records exist to enable us to calculate profits exactly, but it is possible that in normal times the profit made by English merchants in the Flemish market varied between one pound ten shillings and two pounds ten shillings a sack depending upon the quality of the wool. These profits were not high enough to bear customs rates which could rise from the six shillings and eight pence a sack in normal times to forty shillings a sack in wartime. Such rates almost killed the trade in raw wool and caused Flemish weavers to migrate to England and help develop the home cloth industry.

Compared with other Englishmen De la Pole was an intelligent business man, endowed with good judgement and a certain ruthlessness in commercial matters. He had mastered the art of trade and he prospered. His enterprise was as important to Yorkshire as that of the countless monks and laymen who tended the flocks on Yorkshire hillsides.

# Chapter Nine

# THE DEFENCE OF YORKSHIRE IN THE MIDDLE AGES
# CASTLES AT STRATEGIC POINTS

The wooden castles which served to keep the Norman barons safe in their estates soon provided a framework of strong points upon which the defence of the north against the Scots could be based. The Kingdom of Northumbria had once extended as far north as the Firth of Forth. Many Northumbrians were akin to the Scots and it would have been an advantage to the King of Scotland to extend his power as far south as the Humber. The two Kingdoms would then have been of approximately the same size and power. The City of York, the second city of the land, was consequently threatened with capture on several occasions. A defence strategy was required.

To counteract this threat the Norman Kings established powerful noble families, the Percies, Nevilles and Cliffords on vast estates in the north, and created the Bishop of Durham Prince, with extensive administrative responsibilities and military power. The Bishop of Carlisle in the north west was similarly empowered. Castles were built at Carlisle to block the north western approach by way of the Eden Valley, and at Newcastle, Durham, Raby and Barnard Castle to block approaches from Tyne, Wear and Tees. Scarborough protected the entrance from the sea to the Vale of Pickering and Pickering stood mid-way down the Vale beneath the Moors. Each of the passes and dales to the west of the Vale of York was blocked by castles. Brough and Bowes, both built on the original sites of Roman forts, controlled the Stainmore pass. Richmond stood at a superlative strategic point at the lower end of Swaledale. Middleham blocked Wensleydale. Knaresborough stood over the narrow gorge of the Nidd close to the point where it breaks through onto the Vale of York and Skipton, home of the Cliffords, controlled Airedale. York itself was surrounded by its own thick walls and wide ditch. Its gatehouses or 'bars' were each protected by strong barbicans and its citizens were drilled to perform their tasks in defence of the walls. Over the city brooded the mighty castle built round Clifford's tower. As well as this many smaller castles were rebuilt in stone and served as additions to the main strategy. Such were Castle Bolton, home of the Scropes, Sheriff Hutton, a Neville stronghold and Spofforth belonging to the Percies.

The threat of Scottish invasion created a common interest between Norman and Anglian in Yorkshire and brought peasant and lord together as no other cause would have done.

# MIDDLEHAM CASTLE

One of the most impressive of Yorkshire castles is Middleham in Wensleydale. The lands here had been held by Gilpatrick before the Norman Conquest, but in 1069 they were granted to Alan the Red, eldest son of the Count of Penthievre and kinsman to the Duke of Brittany. Alan granted the estates to his brother Ribald in 1089 and they passed through several generations of that family to Ralph Fitzranulph, who died in 1270 without male heir. Thereafter the castle passed in marriage to the Nevilles and was finally surrendered by them to the crown on the death in 1471 of Richard, Earl of Warwick, 'the Kingmaker,' killed in the dense fog which enveloped the Battle of Barnet. King Edward IV granted Middleham to his brother Richard, Duke of Gloucester, afterwards King Richard III. This prince married Warwick's daughter the Lady Anne; and their only son Prince Edward was born in the nursery apartments adjoining the Prince's Tower in the castle. The prince died at Middleham during childhood.

The first castle on the site was a timber motte and bailey erection some 500 yards south west of the present stone castle. Its earthworks are impressive even today. This castle may have been built in 1089 by Ribald and occupation of the site lasted about a hundred years. Work was commenced on the present great rectangular keep by Robert Fitzralph in 1170. When it was complete,the castle consisted of the great keep with inner bailey surrounded by thick curtain walls and wide moat. There was a gatehouse, drawbridge and portcullis and an extensive outer bailey, also surrounded by strong walls and connected to the inner bailey by a second drawbridge, the abutments of which are still in position. The outer bailey is demolished now and its site covered by the buildings of the town. The roofless walls of the keep, gatehouse and inner bailey still stand.

Middleham Castle

## THE CASTLE IN TIME OF WAR

Middleham would have been a difficult castle to attack before the invention of gunpowder. The only way in was by the gatehouse, a machicolated tower three storeys high, with drawbridge to protect the outer face of its vaulted gate-hall and portcullis to block its inner arch. Any invading force would need to fill up the moat with fascines, great bundles of faggots, a difficult task particularly when under fire from the machicolations of the gatehouse and from the battlements of the curtain walls.

If the enemy succeeded in forcing this formidable gatehouse they would be trapped in the gate-hall by the portcullis. Having broken through the portcullis their troubles would not be at an end. Leading soldiers would find themselves in the inner bailey confronted by the massive keep and still under attack from all sides from the battlements above them.

There is no door to the keep at ground level. Access was by outside staircase to a door at first floor level. From this door led the 'screens' passage to The Great Hall, the Chamber of Presence and the Chapel. The staircase was steep and narrow, purposely built in this way to ensure that attackers could not rush it, but would be forced to fight their way up it on the narrowest possible front. Faced with so many difficulties it is small wonder that assaults on such a stronghold were few. A prudent enemy would be more likely to besiege the castle and wait for the defenders to starve, to run-out of water or to die of plague from bad drains and uncleared lavatories.

# THE CASTLE IN TIME OF PEACE

In time of peace Middleham must have witnessed scenes of great pageantry. The arrival of elegantly dressed parties of nobles, knights and ladies, their horses gaily caparisoned, must have been a frequent occurrence. Knights and their retainers serving their duty as castle guard, must have caroused in the great hall, their day's hunting done. The Constable would conduct the business of the estate or entertain important visitors in the chamber of presence, while ladies gossiped over their embroidery in the quiet privy chamber or comfortable nursery. The nursery was placed purposely over the warm bakehouse and was reached from the privy chamber by a wooden bridge so that ladies might not soil their long fur trimmed gowns on the dirty paving of the yard.

On the other side of the keep, adjoining the west wall, the castle priests would celebrate mass in their little chapel and recite the daily office in their pleasant vaulted undercroft.

Round the inner faces of the curtain walls and opening on to the cobbles of the inner bailey were all the offices and

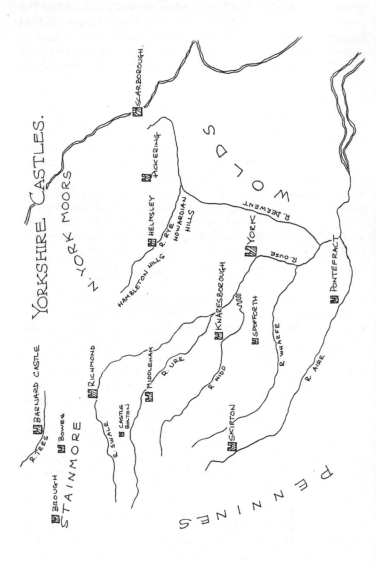

YORKSHIRE CASTLES.

N. YORK MOORS

WOLDS

HAMBLETON HILLS

HOWARDIAN HILLS

STAINMORE

PENNINES

R. TEES
BARNARD CASTLE
BOWES
BROUGH
RICHMOND
CASTLE BOLTON
R. SWALE
MIDDLEHAM
R. URE
KNARESBROUGH
R. NIDD
SKIPTON
SPOFFORTH
R. WHARFE
R. AIRE
PONTEFRACT
R. OUSE
YORK
R. DERWENT
R. RYE
HELMSLEY
PICKERING
SCARBOROUGH

domestic buildings necessary to house those who served the estate and castle in humbler ways. The auditor and his clerks occupied the chambers to the right of the gatehouse, so that they could record the entry and departure of stores wagons of all kinds, horses or cattle. Here too were kept the accounts and rent rolls of all the castle estates. On the west side of the range, beneath the nursery, was the bakehouse with its several round brick ovens and along the south side, past the storage cellars, was a horse-mill for grinding the daily requirement of flour and a brewhouse for making the ale. Middleham had two wells giving fresh water, but ale was the main beverage. Other buildings: slaughter houses, blacksmith's forge, stables, carpenter's shop, cart houses and wheelwright's stores and cattle pens were enclosed within the walls of the outer bailey. A Norman castle was like a small town complete within itself and secure in its own territory.

## THE WARS WITH SCOTLAND

When there was civil war in England or when the English King was weak, attempts were made by the Scots to invade the north. In 1135 King Stephen inherited a troubled kingdom for his cousin, the Empress Matilda a daughter of Henry I, had an equal claim to the throne. Nineteen years of civil war followed. Matilda was supported by King David of Scotland who claimed part of Northumbria for himself. He moved quickly south with an army of wild Galloway men mounted on sturdy ponies and supported by archers. Carlisle was captured and Darlington occupied.

## THE BATTLE OF THE STANDARD

The situation in York seemed desperate, but Archbishop Thurstan, by then a venerable old man, rose to the occasion inspiring courage among the northern nobles and calling-out the fighting men from every parish. Thurstan was only discouraged with some difficulty from leading the army himself. The campaign took on the aspect of a holy war against the pagan Scots who, it had been reported, had carried off the women of Hexham into slavery. Men flocked to the Archbishop's Standard, a ship's mast mounted on a cart supporting the banners of the northern saints: St. Peter of York, St. John of Beverley, St. Wilfrid of Ripon and St. Cuthbert of Durham. On the top of the Standard was a silver 'pyx', a box which contained the consecrated bread and wine of the mass, so that God should accompany the northern army on its mission.

The two armies met at Cowton Moor just north of Northallerton on 22nd August,1138. It was soon after dawn and Thurstan's assistant bishop, the Bishop of Orkney, said mass on the field for the Archbishop's army. The wild charge of the Galloway Scots was checked by the English archers supported by disciplined spearmen,under whose cover they moved forward to retrieve spent arrows. A counter attack by Scottish cavalry led by Prince Henry, son of King David, was repulsed and a mighty struggle ensued in which victory eventually went to the English. King David and Prince Henry escaped to Carlisle. The saintly Ailred, by now Abbot of Rievaulx and himself a Scot, surprisingly had something to comment upon the events of the day. Concerning the charge of his countrymen, the wild Picts of Galloway, he wrote with pride, 'Like a hedgehog with its quills, you might see a Galwegian bristling with arrows with yet a sword still in his hand.' It had been no easy victory for the English.

# THE WHITE FIELD OF MYTON

During the reign of Edward I the fight was taken into Scotland. But after the disgraceful defeat of Edward II at Bannockburn in 1314 the Scots returned to the attack and were met at Myton on Swale in 1319. On this occasion the English were defeated and the battle was remarkable for the large number of clergy killed, their white habits scattering the field like the petals of flowers.

# THE BATTLE OF BOROUGHBRIDGE

Civil war again broke out in 1321 when Warwick and Lancaster and the Lords: Mowbray, Clifford, Amory and Hereford rebelled against Edward II and besieged the royal castle at Tickhill near Doncaster. The Scots joined forces with the rebels and on the 16th March, 1322, the combined forces reached the river Ure at Boroughbridge.

Sir Andrew Harcla, the King's warden at Carlisle, remained loyal and came speedily south with his archers and spearmen placing them to cover the bridge over the Ure and the ford at Milby nearby. The rebel Lancaster attacked the ford with his horsemen,while Clifford and Hereford attacked the bridge with foot soldiers. The fight was keen. Hereford was killed by a spear thrust and Clifford was wounded. Lancaster could make no headway at the ford. A truce was called and the armies encamped for the night. However, early next day Sir Simon de Ward arrived with five hundred reinforcements for Harcla and in the fighting that followed Lancaster was forced back to the church. Many rebel knights escaped in disguise, but Lancaster was captured and taken prisoner to his own castle at Pontefract to be tried for treason. He was later led out on a poor broken-down horse to his execution.

King Edward was triumphant, but the following year the Scots returned and in a skirmish at Byland they routed a small English force. Harcla made peace with the Scots only to be accused of treachery by Edward, tried and painfully executed for his efforts.

The wars with Scotland came temporarily to an end and the people of Yorkshire were relieved of further trouble on this account.

# Chapter Ten

# RELIGIOUS AND CORPORATE LIFE IN A MEDIEVAL CITY

## THE POSITION OF THE CHURCH

The life of medieval man was centred on the church. The services of the church gave joy and comfort to the just. To the repentant sinner there was the promise of forgiveness, but for the unjust, the sinner beyond all help, there was the threat of terrible punishment in hell. Today we seem to have lost much of the faith which inspired medieval man and raised the great and magnificent cathedrals and the many beautiful parish churches we see in Yorkshire. This faith was nurtured by the teaching of inumerable good men, the majority of them simple men, who were the parish priests.

What did the parish priest teach his flock and how did he teach them? The Bible was written in Latin and the prayers of the church were in Latin. The Mass, the principal service of the church was in Latin and only clerks or learned men could read and understand Latin, for as yet there were no bibles in English. Indeed the church would have regarded bible reading by the masses and free discussion of the scriptures as highly dangerous.

## THE PARISH PRIEST

In his description of the poor parson Chaucer gives us a clear picture of the ideal parish priest. First he taught the gospel,after that he led his flock by his own good example. He was kindly, patient, frugal in his own life, but generous to the poor and attentive to the sick. He did not despise sinful men or threaten them, but did his best to draw them towards heaven by fairness. The church, through its sacraments and doctrines provided the means for this.

# THE SACRAMENTS OF THE CHURCH

Man could participate in the seven sacraments of the church and derive much benefit from them. Baptism cleansed him from original sin and made him a Christian. The Holy Eucharist nourished his soul. He received the spirit of the Holy Ghost at his Confirmation as the disciples had done in the upper room at the first Pentecost. The sacrament of Penance gave a chance to retrieve his soul when all might have been lost in sin. Matrimony blessed his earthly union and Unction reconciled his mind to the inevitability of death, or if it were God's will, restored him to health. For the select few, who were to be raised above the laymen as priests, there was also the sacrament of Ordination.

## THE DOCTRINES: THE VIRTUES AND THE ACTS OF MERCY

The priest might teach the three theological virtues: faith, hope and charity. If one had faith, if one lived in hope of eternal life and if one dealt charitably with one's neighbours one would achieve salvation. To govern one's daily life there were the four cardinal virtues: prudence, justice, fortitude and temperance and to regulate one's dealings with other men there were the seven corporal and the seven spiritual acts of mercy. The corporal acts were: to feed the hungry, to give drink to the thirsty, to clothe the naked, to visit the prisoner, to shelter the stranger, to visit the sick and finally to bury the dead. The spiritual acts were: to correct the sinner, to teach the ignorant, to counsel the doubtful, to comfort the sorrowful, to bear wrongs patiently, to forgive all injuries and to pray for the quick and the dead. The virtues and the acts of mercy could be taught without books for they could be seen to work in the daily lives of the people or told in stories of the lives of the saints.

## SIN - THE WORK OF THE DEVIL AND THE CONTRARY VIRTUES

It was the duty of the medieval priest to warn the faithful of the danger of sin. There was 'original sin', into which all men are born to be relieved by baptism, and actual sin which is committed wilfully. The latter could be divided into 'mortal sin', which placed the soul in grave danger, and 'venial sin', which could be more easily relieved. The seven capital sins were: pride, covetousness, lust, anger, gluttony, envy and sloth. The seven contrary virtues, which could help to resist sin were: humility, liberality, chastity, meekness, temperance, brotherly love and diligence. The Christian might also achieve salvation by practising the three eminent good works: giving alms, praying and fasting. It was the priest's duty to explain this.

## PRACTICAL AIDS TO TEACHING

Such was the teaching of the medieval church in place of scripture reading and discussion. It was a practical scheme with guide lines which could be taught practically. Within the church building were usually to be found all the visual aids necessary to illustrate the priest's sermons. Today they have been removed from most churches as idolatrous or unnecessary decoration, but in one city church in York, the Church of All Saints' North Street, a number fortuitously remain. In any medieval city all the churches must once have been furnished as this one is.

## ALL SAINTS' NORTH STREET, YORK

Dividing the screened chancel from the nave is the rood screen, showing the crucifixion of the Saviour, and in the corbels of the barrel-vaulted roof of the chancel are to be seen angels carved in wood and highly coloured. These angels, together with small winged and disembodied angelic heads, suspended over the crucifiction scene, illustrate the constant praise due to God in heaven. A famous stained glass window shows the nine orders of angels: seraphin, cherubin, thrones, dominions, princedoms, powers, virtues, archangels and angels depicted in order of rank. Rank and class were accepted in the medieval world and the heavenly world, if it was to be understood, must reflect this earthly order.

Another window shows the martyr Archbishop Thomas Becket celebrating mass, while the Holy Ghost hovers above, and there is a window to show in graphic form the way in which the seven corporal acts of mercy should be performed. But perhaps the most remarkable window remaining is one named the 'Pricke of Conscience' after a poem, written in the 14th century, by Yorkshireman Richard Rolle of Hampole. The window tells the fate to befall the world in the last fourteen days before judgement day. The stars fall from the heavens; the firmament breaks up in fire and flood; there are strange sea monsters seeming to portray evolution in reverse and in the last panels graves open to give up their dead to the pains of hell, the anguish of purgatory and the joys of heaven.

What the medieval priest lacked in books he surely made up in other ways. Some of the windows, pictures or ornaments he used to illustrate his sermons may still remain in your church. They should not be seen as separate items but as part of a collection which once both beautified the church and made the Christian message intelligible to mortal man.

All Saints' North Street

# THE FREEMEN OF YORK

Medieval cities were often self governing. The right to govern was granted by the King and written down in a charter. A large sum of money would usually be paid for a charter and a further sum for confirmation of the charter.

The city authorities who purchased the charter and who undertook to govern and regulate the city were the freemen. Freemen's rolls in York go back to 1272 but there were freemen long before this date. The Domesday Book mentions the burgesses of York. These were freemen in 1086.

The first Royal Charter for the City of York was dated at some time between 1155 and 1162,when Thomas Becket was Henry II's Chancellor. The charter was negotiated by the freemen, the 'responsible' citizens of York of that time. Freemen were the only persons able to hold municipal office or to vote in the choice of members to attend parliament. They owned the city strays and regulated the rights of pasture upon them. Quite clearly if one wished to be important at all in city affairs one must be a freeman.

There were several ways of achieving freeman status. The first was by 'servitude.' This required an apprentice to serve an indentured apprenticeship of not less than five years in the house and workshop of a freeman who was himself a master craftsman. Another way was by 'patrimony,' a claim by birth right of all sons and grandsons of freemen. Young men, on attaining the age of twenty one, would be invited to the Admissions Court, presided over by the Mayor, and having been identified by an elder blood relation, they would recite the Freeman's Declaration and the Ancient Oath of Obedience and then be admitted as freemen.

A third way of becoming a freeman was by right of 'redemption' or purchase. At a time when those achieving freeman status by 'servitude' paid a fee of six shillings and when those who became freemen by 'patrimony' paid one shilling 'strangers' purchasing their freeman status paid two pounds, often by instalments.

The control which freemen exercised over the government and trade of the city meant that certain established families had great power. This was not always a good thing because the city needed the stimulus of new people and new skills from time to time. On occasion therefore freeman status could be granted to a 'stranger' who was a master craftsman in some particular trade which had died-out in the city, or which the other freemen wished to encourage in the city. In this case often a masterpiece made by the new freeman would be presented to the gild instead of a fee. There are also isolated instances of the Freedom of the City being granted as an honorary award to certain important people. Such was the award to John Kendall in 1483. Kendall was secretary to King Richard III, whom the citizens of York supported.

Freemen governed the city until 1835 when the Municipal Reform Act took away most of their powers and vested them in elected Municipal Corporations. The Gild of Freemen however still exists and meets in its Court House at St. William's College and in the Bedern Hall or attends church at All Saints' Pavement the City Church of the Gild. Freemen still control the pasture rights on the strays and perform certain charitable and ceremonial functions in the city. To be a freeman is considered an honour and freemen from abroad often return to the gild to meet their fellows. Many towns and cities in Yorkshire were once governed by their own freemen. Can you discover anything about the freemen of your own town or city?

# THE RELIGIOUS MERCHANT AND CRAFT GILDS

The religious gilds are probably older than the merchant and craft gilds, for the citizens met for social and religious purposes first. St. Anthony's Hall in York was where the religious Gilds of Corpus Christi, St. Christopher and St. George met. These gilds were very much concerned with the Mystery Plays.

The first craft gild was the Weavers' Gild, which obtained its charter in 1164 from Henry II. By the end of the Middle Ages some eighty separate gilds controlled the admission of craftsmen and merchants, approved the work of apprentices and ensured the quality of merchandise for a radius of some thirty-two miles round York. Today the Butchers' Gild, the Merchant Adventurers, the Guild of Building and the Company of Cordwainers are all active, but active only in social and charitable matters.The Guild of Builders and the Company of Cordwainers also meet in the newly restored Bedern Hall. To a medieval tradesman or master craftsmen membership of his gild was of supreme importance. Gild members and the apprentices, who aspired one day to membership, lived and worked together in the same close packed streets in the city. They sat together at religious feasts and they respected each other's honour in the markets. They acted together in the Mystery Plays and stood together in defence of the walls of the city if necessary. They respected honesty and fair dealing. They buried departed members with dignity, lit candles in the gild churches for the comfort of their souls and they cared for the widows and orphans left behind.

Unhappily, though the gilds were many, the existing records of their doings are few.

A Merchant's House Mulberry Hall

# THE MYSTERY PLAYS - PREPARATIONS FOR THE PLAYS

In June 1397 the whole city of York buzzed in anticipation. For days the streets had been swept and laid with clean rushes. Shrubs and branches fixed in pots and boxes were placed in groups at doorways and silken banners fluttered from windows and corners. It was the Feast of Corpus Christi. The city was full of visitors and,on Toft Green,wainwrights and blacksmiths greased the axles of the great pageant wagons, repainted the scenery upon them or simply repaired the damage of last year's performances. Elsewhere a multitude of sewing women worked at the costumes, marvellously embroidered with peacocks, popinjays and heraldic devices, or starkly simple in homespun broadcloth or fleece. Producers and directors, actors, prompters and scribes laboured over scripts and stage directions; and those with little else to do baked and cooked for the visitors.

Mystery Play

The Corpus Christi Pageant of 1397 was to be an extra special occasion for King Richard II, a great patron of the arts, was to witness the performances. The young King was seated with his fashionable entourage at the gate of the Priory Church of Holy Trinity Micklegate, when the first cart rumbled from nearby Toft Green,to show the story of the Creation enacted by the tanners. God the Father ruled in heaven for a few brief moments over night and day and Lucifer fell from grace, before the cart rumbled off down-hill towards Robert Harphain's door, where the play was re-enacted to the delight of the crowd assembled there. Meanwhile the King was entertained in succession by:the cardmakers and plasterers telling the story of Adam and Eve, by the fullers giving God's dire warning not to touch the fruit of the forbidden tree and by the coopers telling the story of Eve's temptation by Satan and her betrayal of Adam.

# THE ROUTE TAKEN BY THE PAGEANT WAGONS

There were forty-eight plays to see and each was performed twelve times during the day as the pageant wagons passed down Micklegate, over the Old Ouse Bridge, along Spurriergate,Coney Street, Stonegate and Petergate towards the cobbled market place called The Pavement, halting at the appropriate places for their performances. The plays commenced at dawn and continued to dusk,when the stirring spectacle of the Judgement Day, enacted and paid for by the richest of all the gilds, the Merchant Adventurers, was performed for the last time under the walls of the church of All Saints'. The pageant wagons followed each other closely, and there must have been frequent queues, as for example when the very short play of the tylers, about the shepherds and the angel, with its one hundred and fifty lines caught up with the pewterers acting out the three hundred and six lines of Joseph's Dream, or when perhaps the straining labourers just failed to edge their cumbersome wagons neatly round the sharp corners of the narrow streets and jammed them.

# Route Taken By The Pageant Wagons

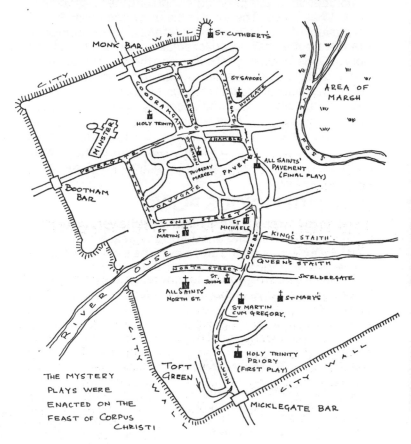

CITY WALL

MONK BAR

St CUTHBERT'S

ALDWARK

St ANDREWGATE

St SAVIOURS

JUBBERGATE

GOODRAMGATE

AREA OF MARSH

HOLY TRINITY

RIVER FOSS

MINSTER

SHAMBLE

PETERGATE

St SAMPSON

ALL SAINTS' PAVEMENT (FINAL PLAY)

THURSDAY MARKET

PAVEMENT

BOOTHAM BAR

STONEGATE

DAVYGATE

CONEY STREET

St MARTINS

St MICHAEL

KING'S STAITH

RIVER OUSE

NORTH STREET

OUSE BR

QUEEN'S STAITH

St JOHNS

SKELDERGATE

ALL SAINTS' NORTH ST.

St MARY'S

St MARTIN CUM GREGORY.

CITY WALL

TOFT GREEN

MICKLEGATE

HOLY TRINITY PRIORY (FIRST PLAY)

CITY WALL

MICKLEGATE BAR

THE MYSTERY PLAYS WERE ENACTED ON THE FEAST OF CORPUS CHRISTI

123

# PLAYS APPROPRIATE TO EACH GILD

The masons and goldsmiths combined to provide the sumptuous spectacle of Herod's Court and the entertainment of the Wise Kings. The locksmiths' play dealt with Satan's temptation of Jesus in the wilderness. The capmakers, plumbers, pattenmakers, pouchemakers and botellers did the story of Christ's ministry in Galilee and the skinners acted the triumphant entry to Jerusalem on the first Palm Sunday. The story of the betrayal and trial of Jesus, his glorious resurrection and the judgement followed scene by scene provided by: cutlers, cordwainers, bowyers and fletchers, tapiters and couchers, cooks and water leders, tile makers, pynners, latoners and painters, butchers, saddlers, winedrawers, carpenters, escreveners, taylors and finally the Merchant Adventurers.

# OTHER RELIGIOUS PLAYS

The annual Corpus Christi Plays were the very highlight of the religious life of the city, enacted to the great expense of the gilds. But they were not the only plays. The story of St. George was played each Midsummer and the Paternoster Gild existed solely for the purpose of their annual play to explain the meaning of the Lord's Prayer. At Lammas every tenth year the story of the creed was produced. This too was witnessed by another King Richard, this time the third, when he visited the city soon after his accession in 1483.

# BEVERLEY AND WAKEFIELD

Mystery plays were performed elsewhere in England and in Yorkshire. At Beverley they took place in the church yard of St. John's. In 1220 we are told by the chronicler, a boy, like Zaccheus in the Bible, climbed up, this time into the triforium of St. John's Minster to get a better view. He fell to the ground apparently lifeless and was preserved only by the miraculous intervention of the Patron Saint. At Wakefield the cycle of plays similar to those of York, included thirty scenes to be performed in the streets. Few manuscripts of these plays exist today for during the religious upheaval of the reformation the scripts were examined by unsympathetic reformers and often condemned as idolatrous and destroyed. There was no place for religious drama in stern Puritan England.

# INFLUENCE OF THE MYSTERY PLAYS ON THE THEATRE

Medieval man was full of life. The urge to dramatise the Christian story in the action and poetry of the plays could not be denied. If the Reformation put an end to this form of entertainment in the 16th century, no doubt much of the vitality and popularity of the secular theatre in Shakespearian times stems from reminiscences of these stirring cycles of plays.

# DISPUTES

In a tightly packed medieval city life was not all harmony. There were frequent disputes. In York one such dispute concerning jurisdiction of the area outside the city walls known as Bootham, often caused contention between the Abbot of St. Mary's and the City. The Abbot wished to claim jurisdiction over the area primarily to obtain the right to hold a fair at the festival of the Nativity of the Virgin. This would of course take trade away from the city, consequently the citizens claimed Bootham as a suburb or liberty under the jurisdiction of the city. The difference seemed to be settled in 1218 when a Justice of Assize ruled that Bootham was a suburb over which the Abbot had no jurisdiction.

# MURDER

Encroachment continued however. In 1261 the citizens attacked and killed certain of the Abbey servants, who had built houses in Bootham. Abbot Simon de Warwick paid a hundred pounds in compensation, but as a concession the Abbey got permission to build the high wall which to this day encloses its grounds.

# CONTROL OF MARYGATE

In 1352 Archbishop William de Thoresby, who was also the Chancellor of England, was asked to settle matters again between the two parties. Under an agreement signed in 1353 the Abbot recognised the jurisdiction of the city over Bootham, but Marygate, the street leading from Bootham to the river,was declared to belong to the abbey, for the purpose of keeping the abbey walls in good repair and for keeping the ditch clean. In addition servants of the abbey were to be free from arrest in Bootham except for felony and trespass.

All was not well however. In 1337 the Mayor claimed the right of way through Marygate to the landing stage on the Ouse to have a timber ship unloaded. The Bursar of the abbey dug a ditch across the road to prevent carts going down to the quay and removed the rudder of the ship to prevent it steering to another landing place. The Mayor was advised to apply to the abbey for a licence to unload. This was an indignity which rankled.

# FURTHER ENCROACHMENT IN BOOTHAM

The dispute was not ended in the 16th century, for in 1500 we hear of a certain smith, Thomas Kendall, building a house at Bootham under the abbey walls and on land leased to him by the Abbot. When the Mayor objected, the Abbot reminded him that he was quite well empowered to permit building under his walls. The city had raised no objection three years earlier, when in 1497 he had constructed Queen Margaret's Arch. Through this the young daughter of Henry VII had passed, with the dignity due to her rank, from his residence on her way to Newborough Priory, and then on to Scotland to marry King James IV. Had the Abbey not been dissolved some thirty nine years later the disputes may have dragged on to this very day.

If sober citizens and men of the Church could pursue such acrimonious quarrels for so long, there is no doubt that, human nature being as it is, many other disputes great and small added spice to the lives of lesser men, crowded as they were into the tight walls of other medieval cities in Yorkshire. It would be interesting to find out about some of them.

# Chapter Eleven

# YORKSHIRE DURING THE WARS OF THE ROSES

The Wars of the Roses were a conflict between two branches of the royal family, the descendants of Edward III's fourth son, John of Gaunt, Duke of Lancaster, and Edward's fifth son, Edmund, Duke of York. The Duke of Lancaster's badge was a red rose and the Duke of York's a white rose. The wars became a murderous struggle between powerful noble families, each with bands of hired mercenaries and retainers. Despite the dislocation caused by the wars the majority of ordinary folk took no sides and endeavoured to live as normally as possible. Much of the fighting took place in Yorkshire where Percies, Cliffords, Mowbrays and Nevilles used the conflict to settle old scores and seize lands and power at each other's expense.

## THE QUARREL

Edward III was not succeeded by his eldest son the Black Prince, who died too soon, but by his grandson Richard II. As a boy Richard had shown great personal courage at the time of the Peasants' Revolt. Later he proved extravagant and less able as a ruler. He provoked a quarrel with his cousin and most powerful rival, Henry Bolingbroke, son of John of Gaunt. He exiled him, hoping while he was away to gain possession of his lands and so deprive him of power. When John of Gaunt died in 1399 Henry returned, landing at Ravenspur at the mouth of the Humber. He seized Richard, imprisoned him at Pontefract Castle, had him murdered and then accepted the crown from parliament, ruling as Henry IV. There was no other strong contender. His cousin Philippa, daughter of Edward III's third son Lionel, Duke of Clarence, was precluded,since no queen had ruled previously in her own right. Her granddaughter Anne Mortimer did however later marry into the family of the Dukes of York making their claim to the throne stronger.

# THE LANCASTRIAN KINGS

At first the House of Lancaster appeared strong. Henry IV ruled successfully having put down rebellions in Yorkshire at Shipton Moor in 1405 and Bramham Moor in 1408. Archbishop Richard Scrope had been one of the leaders of the first rebellion. He was tried hastily and executed for his part, becoming the first Archbishop to pay for his errors in this way.

Henry V, the second Lancastrian King, proved popular as conqueror of half of France, but in 1422 he died leaving his kingdom to his son Henry VI,who succeeded as a child, a child moreover who grew up subject in manhood to nervous breakdowns and bouts of madness, which made him unfit to rule. To make matters worse he was married to an ambitious, clever, cruel and vengeful queen, Margaret of Anjou.

## THE BEGINNING OF THE WARS

During the reign of Henry VI the English were driven out of France and England fell into disorder as old soldiers returned to offer their services to nobles. When Henry became insane in 1453 Richard Plantagenet, third Duke of York, seemed to be the obvious choice of Regent, since Henry's son, Edward Prince of Wales, was a child. He was opposed by Queen Margaret and when his supporters from the north marched south to the skirmish at St. Albans in 1455, the Wars of the Roses had commenced. A proposal in 1460 that on the death of Henry VI the succession should fall to the House of York further enraged Queen Margaret, since this would disinherit her son Edward. It ensured that the wars would be continued with bitterness.

## THE POWER OF THE NOBLES

The great threat to the Crown and the reason why it was possible to wage war was the immense power of the nobles. By the end of the middle ages many powerful noble families had, by marriage or by other means, concentrated vast estates and powers into their hands. Nowhere were nobles more powerful than in the north, where they had in the past provided the only defence against the Scots. They lived like princes in their great castles surrounded by their own estates. They

# The Houses of York and Lancaster

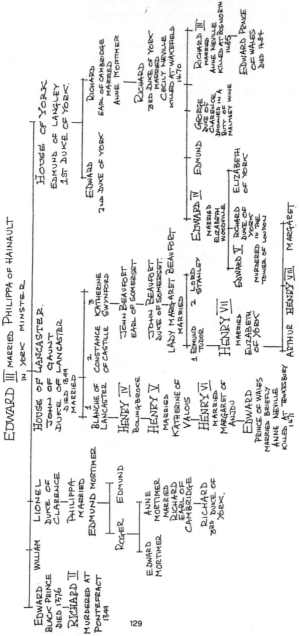

Edward III married Philippa of Hainault in York Minster

**House of Lancaster.** John of Gaunt, Duke of Lancaster, died 1399, married (1) Blanche of Lancaster, (2) Constance of Castile, (3) Katherine Swynford

**House of York.** Edmund of Langley, 1st Duke of York

Edward, Black Prince, died 1376 — Richard II murdered at Pontefract 1399

William

Lionel, Duke of Clarence, married Philippa — Edmund Mortimer — Roger / Edmund; Anne Mortimer married Richard Earl of Cambridge — Richard, 3rd Duke of York; Edward Mortimer

Blanche of Lancaster (1) — Henry IV Bolingbroke — Henry V married Katherine of Valois — Henry VI married Margaret of Anjou — Edward Prince of Wales married briefly Anne Neville killed at Tewkesbury 1471

Katherine Swynford (3) — John Beaufort Earl of Somerset — John Beaufort Duke of Somerset — Lady Margaret Beaufort married (1) Edmund Tudor, (2) Lord Stanley — Henry VII married Elizabeth of York — Arthur; Henry VIII; Margaret

Edward, 2nd Duke of York

Richard Earl of Cambridge married Anne Mortimer — Richard, 3rd Duke of York married Cecily Neville killed at Wakefield 1470 — Edward IV married Elizabeth Woodville; George Duke of Clarence drowned in a butt of malmsey wine; Edmund; Elizabeth of York; Richard III married Anne Neville killed at Bosworth 1485 — Edward Prince of Wales died 1484

Edward IV married Elizabeth Woodville — Edward V murdered in the Tower of London; Richard Duke of York murdered in the Tower of London; Elizabeth of York

YEH—I

129

proclaimed their wealth and pride by their elaborate coats of arms and they supported private armies of retainers: soldiers, stewards, clerks, huntsmen and grooms all clad in their own liveries. They also extended their influence over their tenants, men of intermediate rank, small landowners and such like, by a system of maintenance. This meant that in consideration for support, they promised to maintain the interest of their tenants in law courts or in any conflict with others, thereby undermining the whole fabric of royal government.

# THE PERCIES AND THE NEVILLES

The two most powerful families in Yorkshire were the Percies and the Nevilles. They both had strongholds further north but they had extended their influence south into Yorkshire. The Percies' main estates were in the East Riding at Leconfield and Beverley. In the West Riding they had lands round Spofforth. They were allied by marriage to the Cliffords of Skipton, the Roos of Helmsley, the Dacres, Scropes and Mowbrays.

The Nevilles had Middleham and Sheriff Hutton and through the marriage of the Lady Cecily to Richard Plantagenet third Duke of York, they were allied to the Yorkist line. Richard Neville had married the heiress to the Beauchamp estates in the Midlands and became, as the Earl of Warwick, 'the Kingmaker,' the most powerful noble in England.

# THE STRUGGLE IN YORKSHIRE - THE PERCIES SUPPORT THE LANCASTRIANS

At first the Percies had opposed the seizure of the crown by Henry IV. The Earl and his son, the young Harry Hotspur, were both killed for their part in the two early rebellions in Yorkshire. But the Lancastrian Kings needed the Percies to defend the border with Scotland, and they were left in possession of their estates and became reconciled to the Lancastrians and firm Lancastrian supporters.

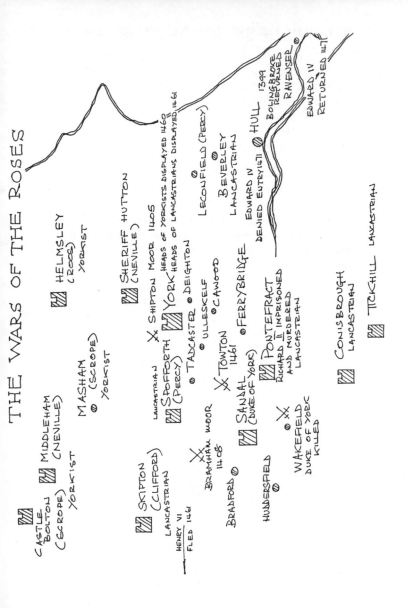

THE WARS OF THE ROSES

CASTLE BOLTON (SCROPE) YORKIST

MIDDLEHAM (NEVILLE) YORKIST

MASHAM (SCROPE) YORKIST

HELMSLEY (ROOS) YORKIST

SHERIFF HUTTON (NEVILLE)

✕ SHIPTON MOOR 1405

SPOFFORTH (PERCY)

YORK HEADS OF YORKISTS DISPLAYED 1460 HEADS OF LANCASTRIANS DISPLAYED 1461

LECONFIELD (PERCY)

BEVERLEY LANCASTRIAN

HULL 1399

EDWARD IV DENIED ENTRY 1471

BOLINGBROKE RETURNED RAVENSER

EDWARD IV RETURNED 1471

LANCASTRIAN

⊙ TADCASTER  ⊙ DEIGHTON

⊙ ULLESKELF

⊙ CAWOOD

SKIPTON (CLIFFORD) LANCASTRIAN

HENRY VI FLED 1461

✕ BRAMHAM MOOR 1408

SANDAL (DUKE OF YORK)

⊙ FERRYBRIDGE

✕ TOWTON 1461

PONTEFRACT RICHARD II IMPRISONED AND MURDERED LANCASTRIAN

⊙ BRADFORD

✕ WAKEFIELD DUKE OF YORK KILLED

CONISBROUGH LANCASTRIAN

⊙ HUDDERSFIELD

TICKHILL LANCASTRIAN

131

# THE NEVILLES SUPPORT THE YORKISTS

The Duke of York had been unable to maintain his position in the south after his early success at St. Albans and had been forced temporarily to leave the country. He returned in 1459 and the Nevilles led their forces to join him in the Midlands. No sooner had they gone than the Percies and other Lancastrians overran Yorkshire.

## QUEEN MARGARET LEADS THE LANCASTRIANS

The Duke of York captured Henry VI at Northampton in 1460 and put forward the claim to the throne which would disinherit the Prince of Wales. But Queen Margaret had joined the Percies in Yorkshire where the Lancastrian position, based on the three great castles of Conisbrough, Pontefract and Tickhill, seemed secure.

York hurried north, where he found Percy holding the crossing of the Aire in strength at Pontefract. He drew back briefly to his castle at Sandal and later rashly allowed himself to be trapped at Wakefield and killed. On the same day his second son Edmund, a teenage boy, was said to have been murdered by Clifford himself. The Yorkists had failed. Queen Margaret had the severed heads of York and the Earl of Salisbury displayed on Micklegate Bar, the main entrance to the City of York. York's head was scornfully decorated with a paper crown so that, as King, he could overlook his northern capital. Then the victorious Lancastrians set off killing and pillaging towards London.

## THE YORKISTS TRIUMPH - EDWARD IV CROWNED

The citizens of London, alarmed by the uncouth behaviour of the Lancastrians, refused the Queen entry and she was forced to return to Yorkshire. On March 4th, 1461, Edward Earl of March, the eighteen year old son of the Duke of York and Cecily Neville was crowned Edward IV.

Micklegate Bar

# TOWTON - A YORKIST VICTORY

The young King proved himself an able general. He hurried north with Warwick, crossed the Aire at Ferrybridge against Clifford's defence and on Palm Sunday, 29th March came up with the main Lancastrian army at Towton. Here the Earl of Warwick, commander of Edward's forces, ordered his charger to be brought to him and, before the astonished soldiery, he killed it with his own hand, vowing that he would fight to the death like any common man. This extraordinary demonstration proved effective. Yorkist morale was high, despite their disadvantage in numbers. A freak snowstorm blew up from the south beating into the faces of the Lancastrians and causing their arrows to fall short. As the Yorkists surged forward they fired the spent Lancastrian arrows back from whence they had come and soon bitter hand to hand fighting developed in the billowing snow. The day was won for Edward when Yorkist reinforcements arrived and the

Lancastrians broke in disorder. Many were drowned crossing the river. When Queen Margaret heard of the defeat she escaped from the City of York to Scotland.

There were changes to be made in the city. The grisly heads of the Yorkists were taken down from Miclklegate Bar and replaced by those of Lancastrian nobles! Edward returned to London in triumph. Parliament declared all lands of the Duchy of Lancaster in the north forfeit to the crown and the King took possession of them. The Nevilles did very well. Warwick's brother John took Percy's lands and title. George Neville became Archbishop of York and Middleham Castle became the home of Richard, the King's rather frail seven-year old brother. Henry VI became a fugitive cared for first by Sir Ralph Pudsey at Bolton-by-Bowland and afterwards by the Singletons of Waddington in Lancashire. Even so his troubles were not over. He was captured by the Yorkist Talbots as he crossed the River Ribble and was sent prisoner to the Tower of London.

# EDWARD AND WARWICK QUARREL

All did not go well between Edward IV and his mainstay Warwick. Warwick was in favour of a royal marriage with a French princess, but the impulsive Edward suddenly married Elizabeth Woodville, the widow of a Lancastrian nobleman, a lady with a number of needy and ambitious relatives. To follow this up Edward embarked on a commercial treaty with Flanders, which was to the advantage of English merchants, but which was not what Warwick would have advised. There was an open quarrel. Warwick found an ally in George, Duke of Clarence, the King's younger brother, who married Isabella Neville, Warwick's daughter. A number of small disturbances occurred in the north, which Warwick ignored, and Edward was obliged to travel north to reinstate his former enemies the Percies to re-establish a balance of power against the Nevilles. The situation got out of hand and Edward fled to Flanders leaving his throne vacant. Warwick changed sides. He travelled to France, where he was reconciled to the old Queen Margaret, saw his younger daughter Anne married to her son Edward Prince of Wales and replaced the now foolish King Henry VI on the throne. But his triumph was short lived.

Edward IV landed again at Ravenspur in March,1471 with a small force. He was denied entry to Hull and Beverley, but he received help from the City of York before hurrying down to London to confront his former ally.

# EDWARD RE-ESTABLISHES THE HOUSE OF YORK

The Lancastrian cause collapsed after the defeats at Barnet, where Warwick was killed, and at Tewkesbury where Edward Prince of Wales met his death and Queen Margaret was captured. Poor Anne Neville, married for such a short time, was a widow at fifteen. At Edward's command the miserable Henry VI was murdered and Yorkist rule was re-established.

The north however was still more turbulent than elsewhere and now Edward found in his brother Richard, now Duke of Gloucester, a trustworthy aide. He was appointed Warden of the Western Marches and steward of the Duchy of Lancaster, responsible for defence against the Scots. In Yorkshire he received the Neville lands. He wished to marry the young widow Anne Neville, whom he had known since childhood in Middleham. He was twenty years old and she was now sixteen. As soon as possible this was accomplished and the young couple travelled to Yorkshire to make their home in Wensleydale at the castle at Middleham. It was probably a love-match, unusual in an age when marriages in the royal family and among the nobility were all arranged for political purposes.

# RICHARD DUKE OF GLOUCESTER - SERVES EDWARD

Much has been written of this prince which is probably not true. According to Shakespeare he was a villainous hunchback steeped in all kinds of treachery, a murderer and a tyrant. Shakespeare based his evidence on a book by Sir Thomas More, Henry VIII's Chancellor. The evidence used by Sir Thomas was pure hearsay and both authors were concerned primarily with supporting the Tudor monarchy and not with historical truth. Only two portraits of Richard III exist and in neither is he shown with gross deformity. Nor are his alleged deformities noted in contemporary descriptions of him. His appearance, like his character, has been blackened by those who supplanted him. He was slight, with an intelligent face and keen eyes. He may have suffered from polio in childhood which could have left him with a small stoop, but this is by no means proven.

Throughout his life he was active and industrious and a good soldier, loyal above all else to his brother King Edward IV. He was a northerner, direct and frugal, unused to the extravagance and intrigue of the Woodvilles at Court. He preferred to live at Middleham, where his son Prince Edward was born, and where he sheltered his wife Anne's mother, the 'Kingmaker's' widow.

By 1482 he had established good terms with the Lancastrian Percy and with his help and that of Lord Dacre, another former Lancastrian, he had pushed back Scottish encroachment and recaptured Berwick-on-Tweed, which had been sold to the Scots by Queen Margaret.

He visited York frequently, accepting ceremonial gifts and acknowledging the loyalty of the city. He and the Lady Anne were admitted to the Corpus Christi Gild and they witnessed the Mystery Plays. The Gild of Freemen deferred to him and his advice was sought in the election of a Lord Mayor. When his brother Clarence, suspected of plotting against King Edward IV, was lodged in the tower, knocked on the head and pitched mysteriously headfirst into a vat of Malmsey wine to drown, he founded a college of chantry priests at Middleham and a second college at Barnard Castle to pray for the King, who had most likely been responsible for the deed.

# GOVERNMENT BY A COUNCIL OF ABLE MEN

Richard established a council of advisers at Sheriff Hutton, similar to the Great Council of the Realm, to administer justice to noble landlords and humble tenants alike. This was a necessary reform when one considers the breakdown in law and order that had accompanied the wars. Its members were: Lord Scrope of Castle Bolton, Sir Richard Radcliffe, Lord

Dacre, Sir James Metcalfe, Lord Lovell and Sir Francis Percy. Some of these were lesser men of the gentry rather than of the old nobility. Sir James Metcalfe was a trained lawyer. This was a fore-shadowing of the Tudor system of government. The council at Sheriff Hutton became responsible for defence, justice and all aspects of administration. Later it was to be removed to York and to become the Council of the North under a Lord President.

# RICHARD BECOMES KING

Edward IV died on 9th April, 1483 leaving his son and heir the twelve year old Edward V, and his younger brother Richard, Duke of York, to the care of the Duke of Gloucester as 'Protector.' The boys were under the influence at Court of the Woodvilles, Richard's enemies. The situation was full of danger. Richard struck first imprisoning Lord Rivers the Queen's brother, Grey her son by her former marriage, and Vaughan her adviser. He made at the same time his own claim to the throne on the grounds that his brother's marriage to Elizabeth Woodville had been invalid.

Richard's reasons for this were sensational. Evidence had been brought to him by the Bishop of Bath and Wells, by now a cleric with a troubled conscience, that King Edward had been married secretly, in the first year of his reign, to the Lady Eleanor Butler, Lord Talbot's daughter. The Bishop, then a young priest, claimed to have solemnized the marriage himself. If this were so, Edward's marriage to his Queen Elizabeth Woodville was illegal and the princes were bastards with no claim to the throne. The unfortunate Lady Eleanor, Edward's first wife, had been dead for some years having spent a good deal of her life languishing quietly with a strange melancholy in a Carmelite nunnery in Norwich. She would therefore be unable to give evidence herself. To compound the matter it was also reported to Richard that the dead King had been bewitched by Jacquetta, Elizabeth Woodville's mother. The two women, mother and daughter, were said to have practised black magic to win Edward's love. It was sufficient to blacken the princes. The two boys were lodged in the Tower soon to disappear from the pages of history. They were murdered, by whom and when we do not really know, despite recent expert examination of their mortal remains. These should be compared with those of the tiny Anne Mowbray, daughter of the Duke of Norfolk and heiress to his vast estates. She had been married to the younger of the two princes in 1478, when she was only five and he a few months younger. She died at Greenwich in 1481 just before reaching her ninth birthday. Any significant disparity between the size of the young Duke of York's bones and those of his little wife might indicate that his death could have taken place some time after the time commonly accepted. A great disparity might even point to a date after 1485 when Richard III was dead and Henry VII was King.

Richard and Anne Neville were crowned in 1483. There were few disorders. The new King was supported by several thousand northern troops, some three hundred of whom came from the City of York with the two members of Parliament from the city. Their armour was rusty and their manner and appearance rough, but their loyalty was unquestionable. After the coronation they were sent home and the new King and Queen began a progress through the country dispensing justice. In York the young Prince Edward, their son, was invested in the Minster Library as Prince of Wales. Everything seemed to have been accomplished with the minimum of trouble.

# THE FINAL CAMPAIGN

In 1484 the first disaster struck the royal couple. Prince Edward died. He was buried in the parish church of Sheriff Hutton. But now the succession to the throne was again uncertain and rival claimants began their preparations. A rebellion in support of the Duke of Buckingham was suppressed in the south west. The main danger however came from Henry Tudor, Earl of Richmond. He was son of Lady Margaret Beaufort, a descendent of John of Gaunt and Katherine Swynford. She was married to Lord Stanley who had vast estates in Lancashire and was ruler of the Isle of Man. Henry was also descended from Catherine of Valois, widow of Henry V by her second marriage to a Welsh gentleman, Owain Tudor.

Henry Tudor was in Brittany. There he collected supporters for his bid for the throne: old Lancastrian supporters, Woodvilles and remnants of the old nobility who disliked Richard's form of government, which favoured the gentry rather than the nobles.

A second blow fell upon Richard when his Queen Anne died in March, 1485. In August the Earl of Richmond landed at Milford Haven and began his march through Wales collecting any who would help him.

Richard issued 'commissions of array' calling upon all able-bodied men to support him. Scrope, Dacre and Greystone joined him. Percy commanded his own followers. Lord Lovell brought the Midland Levies and John Howard, Duke of Norfolk, those from East Anglia. Richard's army was large, and unlike the forces of earlier battles in the Wars of the Roses, was not made up entirely of the retainers of the magnates, but contained a high proportion of free men, who had answered the royal call.

The battle of Bosworth was settled by two defections. Percy, whose forces were in the rear of Richard's army, drew back and played no part. Lord Stanley, who should in loyalty have joined Richard with the levies from Lancashire and Cheshire, led his men to support Henry Tudor, who thereby gained preponderance on the battlefield. The Yorkists fought staunchly and Richard, risking everything on a personal encounter with his adversary, cut his way through towards the place where Henry Tudor was standing. He was almost upon him when he was himself struck down. The crown of England is said to have rolled under a thorn bush from which it was picked up and offered to Henry.

# AFTERMATH

Even so, there were many who regretted the death of Richard. The eighty staunch men of the City of York who arrived at Bosworth Field too late for the fighting, returned with heavy hearts to place their sorrow on record. In the House Books of York Corporation on 23rd August, 1485 appears a minute that gives proof that King Richard was liked and respected. It reads thus: 'King Richard, late mercifully reigning upon us, was through grete treason ..... piteously slane and murdered to the grete hevynesse of this Citie ......'

# THE HOUSE OF TUDOR

Henry Tudor,who ruled as Henry VII,lost no time in joining the houses of York and Lancaster in marriage. On January 18th, 1486 he married Elizabeth, daughter of Edward IV and the senior claimant of the Yorkist line. The two roses were combined in the new Tudor Rose. The first king to unite the Houses by birth was their son Henry VIII.

In the north a general pardon was issued to the Yorkists, whose co-operation was now needed to counter any threat from the Scots. Percy, Dacre and Scrope retained their offices. Clifford the Lancastrian regained his estates. The Nevilles had gone for ever and their lands were taken by the Crown. In the next reign the power of the great barons was to be curbed effectively by the statutes against maintenance and liveries. Cases against even the mightiest subjects were to be heard in the Star Chamber or before the Council of the North in York. Smaller men need fear great oppressors much less than before.

# EVERYDAY LIFE IN YORKSHIRE DURING THE WARS

While the wars were plunging parts of the north into disorder there were other places where life went on much as usual. The monasteries, and there were many in Yorkshire, remained secure. When tenants of lay estates were forced to go off to fight, abbey tenants stayed at home giving stability to the countryside and producing iron, lead, wool and grain for trade or export.

In the West Riding Dales in the 15th century,the running water of the Pennine streams was being used more widely to power small fulling mills. Its softness made it ideal for washing, dyeing and other processes in the cloth trade which entered a period of prosperity. Small West Riding towns, Wakefield, Huddersfield, Bradford and others had an advantage over York and Beverley, older cloth producing areas, where gild

Merchant Taylors' Hall

restrictions were beginning to hamper the trade by forcing prices too high. There was a beginning of church building and reconstruction, though not on the scale of the Cotswold builders or those of East Anglia.

We have seen that cities, safe behind their walls, were able on occasion to defy kings and refuse them entry. It was a period when civic pride flourished and merchant and craft gild halls were built. In 1444 the Great Gildhall overlooking the Ouse in York was completed as a fitting court for the Lord Mayor and Council. St. Anthony's Hall was built for the carpenters and saddlers in 1446 and the Merchant Taylors' Hall is of much the same age.

The great east window of York Minster had been put in by John Thornton, master glazier of Coventry, at a cost of fifty five pounds between 1406 and 1409 at the beginning of the period of the wars. The two western bell towers of the Minster and the great central tower were completed in 1472 during the wars. Much of the medieval woodcarving and illuminating was in position The two master craftsmen who did the superb carving of the beams and bosses of the central tower ceilings, so splendidly restored and revealed today, were James Damm, a Flemming, and David the Carver. Damm was made a Freeman of York and paid forty five shillings for his nine week's carving. David received a bonus of ten shillings from the Dean and Chapter in addition to the seventeen and fourpence contract price for his labour. Work on the ceiling joists had been put in hand two years previously when forty six great oaks were brought from Ulleskelf down the Wharfe and Ouse to York. There had been seventeen joiners engaged on the roof work at that time and the demand for timber had kept the men of Ulleskelf, Deighton and Cawood hard at work cutting and carting.

The painting and gilding of the tower ceiling used thirty one thousand leaves of beaten gold, two casks of linseed oil a large quantity of blue, vermilion, red lead, white lead, ochre and varnish. Masons had worked from sunrise to dusk for years, with respite on saints' days, to complete the Cathedral, and now that the task was finished, there was little fear of redundancy. Repairs to the vast structure were expected to keep local craftsmen at work for years to come. Such an undertaking must demonstrate the general prosperity of the time.

In the centre of the city the Church of All Saints' was rebuilt with a high lantern tower to guide travellers approaching from the Forest of Galtres and close under the walls of the minster the beautiful Court of St. William's College was built to house the Chantry Priests.

In every city the war provided no real setbacks to improvement. Hull flourished as a Port. The craft gilds of Beverley rebuilt the nave of St. Mary's church and in Ripon the central tower of the Minster was reconstructed. Elsewhere, in towns where there were no cathedral-schools: Wakefield, Pontefract, Pickering, Pocklington, Northallerton and Skipton, Grammar Schools were founded. Yorkshire folk clearly permitted the wars to affect their lives as little as possible.